DATE DUE

Silver Burdett Picture Histories

The Barbarian Invasions of Europe

Patrick Périn and Pierre Forni
assisted by Laure-Charlotte Feffer

Illustrated by Pierre Joubert

Translated by Nan Buranelli

Library of Congress Cataloging-in-Publication Data

Périn, Patrick.
   The Barbarian invasions of Europe.

   (Silver Burdett picture histories)
   Translation of: Au temps des royaumes barbares.
   Summary: Surveys the Germanic barbarian tribes that
proliferated in Europe at the end of the Roman Empire
and describes how their social life and customs formed
the basis for early medieval civilization.
      1. Migration of nations—Juvenile literature.
2. Rome—History—Germanic invasions, 3rd–6th centuries—
Juvenile literature.   3. Europe—History—476-1492—
Juvenile literature.   [1. Europe—History—476-1492.
2. Rome—History—Germanic invasions, 3d–6th centuries.
3. Civilization, Medieval.   4. Middle Ages]   I. Forni,
Pierre.   II. Title.   III. Series.
D135.P4713   1986   940.1   86-61628
ISBN 0-382-09394-1

Impreso por: Edime Org. Gráfica, S. A. Móstoles (Madrid)
Encuaderna: Larmor, S. A. Móstoles (Madrid)
Depósito legal: M. 14.530-1987
I.S.B.N.: 599-1970-6
Impreso en España - Printed in Spain

First published in France in 1984 by Librairie Hachette, Paris
as *La Vie privée des Hommes: Au temps des royaumes barbares.*

First published in the United States in 1987 by
Silver Burdett Press, Morristown, New Jersey

Contents

From the Goths to Charlemagne

(fifth-eighth centuries)

The Great Barbarian Invasions of Europe began in the fifth century A.D. By this time, Rome had existed for a thousand years. From the City on the Seven Hills, an immense empire had grown. For a long time, it was the only great power of the Mediterranean world.

In order to build ever more splendid monuments, feed its enormous population, and its half million soldiers, the Roman Empire constantly had to keep pushing its frontiers outward. It did so successfully through the second century A.D., conquering entire kingdoms in western Asia and North Africa. Elsewhere it held in check the barbarians—the peoples who never founded big cities, such as the Celts, the Germans, the Alani, and the Berbers.

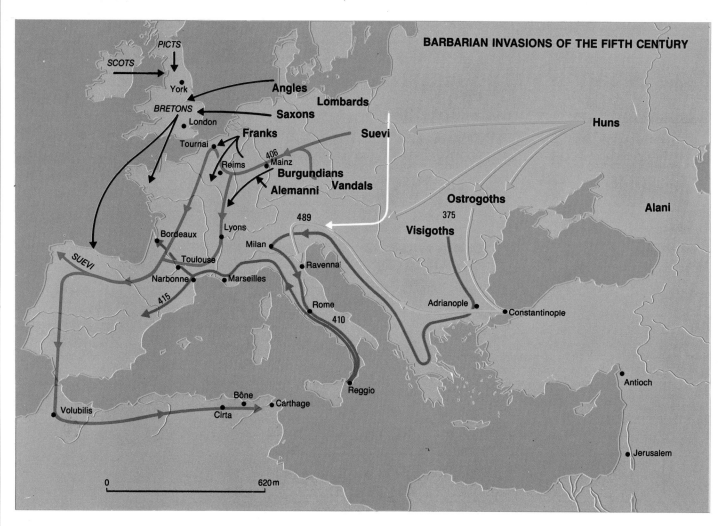

BARBARIAN INVASIONS OF THE FIFTH CENTURY

BARBARIANS IN THE EMPIRE

Beginning in the third century, the Romans faced more and more difficulties. Unable to raise troops from among their own citizens, the eastern emperors Diocletian and Constantine decided to hire auxiliary soldiers from among the barbarians, mainly Germans. Some were forced to serve in the military, having been compelled to settle within the empire as farmers after being conquered. They were called *Letes* (meaning "bound"). Others, after signing treaties, freely entered the service of Rome as whole tribes. They were called *Foederati* (from the Latin *foedus,* "treaty"). Both the *Letes* and the *Foederati* were responsible for defending the natural frontiers of the Rhine and the Danube, to the north and east of the empire. Sometimes barbarian soldiers made brilliant careers in the Roman armies because of their military ability. Those who became commanding generals included a Vandal, Stilicho, and Arbogast, a Frank.

A MOSAIC OF PEOPLES: THE GERMANS

In the fourth century, a multitude of barbarian peoples held an immense territory extending north of the Roman and Persian empires. The majority of them were German.

The Salian Franks, named for the Sala (modern Ijssel) River, occupied lands from north of the Rhine to what is today southwest Belgium. The Franks along the Rhine, called Ripuarians (from the Latin word *ripa,* meaning "riverbank"), held the middle Rhine near the cities of Cologne and Mainz. They were in contact with the Burgundians, who had recently arrived from the distant shores of the Baltic Sea. The Alemanni occupied the land between the Main River and the headwaters of the Rhine and Danube; they were neighbors of the Thuringians and the Bavarians. The Saxons and the Lombards lived in northern Germany; the Angles and Jutes in Denmark; from the Baltic south to the lower Danube lived the Suevi, Lombards, Vandals, Gepids, and Visigoths (west Goths). The Ostrogoths (east Goths) were established north of the Black Sea; their neighbors to the east were Iranian nomads, the Alani and the Sarmatians. Farther east lay the world of the Huns, nomads from central Asia.

These barbarians were unable to unite, even though they faced an empire whose wealth they coveted. They fought incessant wars with one another to defend the lands to which chance or their migrations had led them. Even people of the same tribe did not hesitate to fight one another in order to impose their own chief over the whole community. The barbarians had a deserved reputation as ferocious warriors.

In spite of their conflicts, the Germans had in common their traditions, language, and habits of thought. They lived by farming and herding, but also traded and made handicrafts. There was unquestionably a Germanic civilization. German smiths, for example, forged formidable weapons, better than anyone had ever produced before.

A ring of Childeric I, the father of Clovis. Discovered in 1653 at Tournai, near the church of Saint Brice, the ring enabled scholars to identify the tomb of the Frankish king. The inscription, CHILDIRICI REGE, is visible on the front of what was a royal seal. The king, who is shown clad in a cuirass (breast-plate), wears a cape over his shoulders; according to the royal tradition of the Franks, he has long braided hair. In his right hand he holds a lance, the symbol of his power. (Collection of Medals, Bibliothèque Nationale, Paris)

Objects from the tomb of Childeric. Decorations of inlaid gold from a sword hilt and the top of its sheath, discovered in 1653. (Collection of Medals, Bibliothèque Nationale, Paris)

The technique and extraordinary ability of their craftsmen produced marvelous works of art: colored gems and skillfully wrought stylized animals.

Each people was organized into tribes and clans. Supreme power belonged to elected war chieftains. Many slaves (mostly prisoners of war) lived under the authority of free men. The chiefs set up laws based on custom and oral tradition.

The Germans worshiped not only the forces of nature but also many deities. These included Wotan, the god of war, and Freya, goddess of the family.

THE HUNS IN EUROPE: BEGINNING OF THE GREAT INVASIONS

In the fourth century, the western Huns marched from Asia toward Europe, driving other barbarian peoples westward. This event, without precedent in history, began the movement known as the Great Invasions, or Great Migrations.

Since the beginning of the Christian era, the Huns had lived in the region between the Aral Sea and Lake Baikal. First, they migrated toward the east, only to be halted by the powerful Chinese Empire. Beginning about 350 A.D., they moved onto the steppes north of the Caspian and Black seas, where the Sarmatians and the Alani were living. Some twenty years later, they collided with the Goths, whom they defeated decisively in 375. Most of the Visigoths crossed the Danube and asked for asylum from Valens, the eastern Roman emperor. The Ostrogoths submitted to the Huns and remained under their control until the mid-400s.

PEOPLES ON THE MOVE

Although the Visigoths obtained the status of *Foederati* from Valens, they were quick to betray him. On August 9, 378, they crushed his army at Adrianople. They then began a long journey. Established in northern Greece and what is now Yugoslavia, the Visigoths invaded Italy in 401. They took Rome and sacked it in 410. They captured Galla Placidia, the sister of the emperor Theodosius. To Romans of the western empire, these events clearly heralded the beginning of the end. As for the Visigoths, they then turned northward and invaded Gaul; present-day France.

Meanwhile, after forcing the Visigoths to flee and subjugating the Ostrogoths, the Huns occupied Hungary in 405 and drove the Germans out. The Alani, Suevi, and Vandals, fleeing west, took advantage of an exceptionally cold winter to cross the frozen Rhine near Mainz on December 31, 406. For almost three years they ravaged Roman Gaul. Some Alani remained there, settling along the middle Loire as *Foederati,* with the permission of the Roman authorities. Others continued, with the Suevi and the Vandals, into Spain. The Suevi stopped there, but the Vandals left in 429 for North Africa under the leadership of their king, Genseric (who died in 477).

The mausoleum of Theodoric the Great (493–526) at Ravenna, early sixth century. This curious monument, unlike anything else in the West, held the remains of the greatest of the Ostrogothic kings, whose capital was at Ravenna.

Seal of King Alaric II (484–507). This photograph of the impression made by the seal clearly shows the inscription, ALARICUS REX GOTHORUM. The king of the Visigoths is portrayed in the ancient style, with his head uncovered and wearing a cuirass. (Kunsthistoriches Museum, Vienna)

THE BARBARIANS IN GAUL

Other Germanic peoples took advantage of the chaotic circumstances to invade Gaul and establish themselves there, although they did so in a less brutal manner than the Alani, Suevi, and Vandals. The Salian Franks moved quickly as far as the Somme. The Alemanni reached Alsace and eastern Switzerland. The Burgundians, defeated by the Huns in 436 and forced to leave their kingdom at Worms, arrived in 443 in Roman Switzerland and in the southern region of the Jura Mountains as *Foederati*. The constantly moving Visigoths arrived on the banks of the Garonne River, also with the status of *Foederati*, and began their conquest of Aquitaine.

In spite of all these disturbances, the Roman Empire of the West managed to survive for a few more decades. Under the Emperors Honorius (395–423) and Valentinian III (433–455), Italy rose from the ruins left by the invading Visigoths. In Gaul, a Roman leader named Aetius gained control of the situation. This representative of the emperor, born a Roman, but reared among the Visigoths and then the Huns (who held him as a hostage), compelled respect for the treaties between Rome and the barbarians established in Gaul: the Franks, the Burgundians, and the Visigoths. When the Huns threatened the West for the last time, it was Aetius who organized its defense. He mobilized Visigoths, Franks, Burgundians, Alani, and Saxons, and crushed Attila and his Huns near Troyes in 451.

Gaul was also invaded from Britain, to the west. The Romans had abandoned Britain in 407 under pressure from the Celtic Picts and Scots. The island was then invaded by Germanic peoples—the Jutes, Angles, and Saxons—from northern Europe. Their invasions in turn displaced the Celtic Britons. Beginning in the mid-400s, many of them crossed over to the continent and settled in Armorica (Brittany), where they reinforced the Celtic people already there.

BIRTH OF THE BARBARIAN KINGDOMS

From the mid-fifth century on, the main barbarian peoples began to settle down in more or less fixed territories. Little by little, they created kingdoms out of the debris of the Roman Empire in the West.

Italy was the scene of several invasions. The Huns had fallen upon it after their defeat in Gaul. They did not remain long, and Attila died in 453. By this time, however, the direction of the Roman Empire was effectively in the hands of Germanic barbarians.

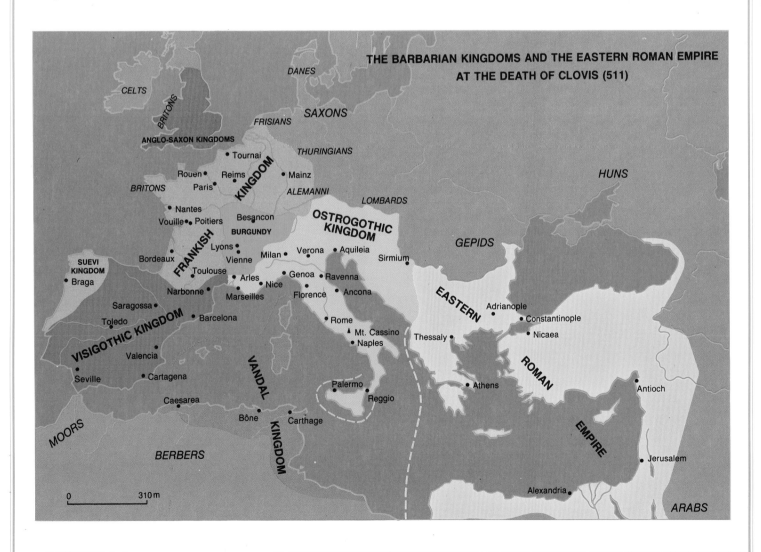

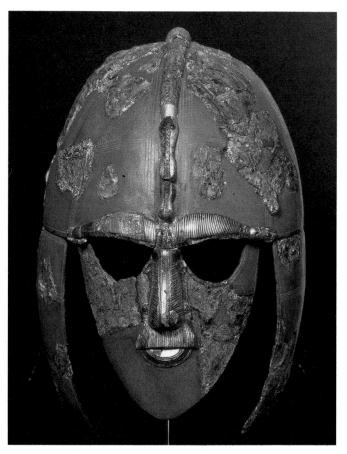

Helmet of King Redwald (died about 625). The tomb of this Anglo-Saxon king of East Anglia, placed in a ship according to Scandinavian custom, was discovered at Sutton Hoo (Suffolk) in 1939. One of the most spectacular objects among the sumptuous burial objects was this iron helmet decorated with gilded bronze and inlaid ornamentation. Based on tournament helmets from late antiquity, with its face protection in the form of a mask, it is related to contemporary Viking helmets used in eastern Scandinavia. (British Museum, London)

One of them, Odoacer, removed the last Roman emperor, Romulus Augustulus, who was still a child. This event, in 476, officially marks the end of the Roman Empire in the West.

The Ostrogoths were next on the scene. They had liberated themselves from the Huns after Attila's death. They had then threatened the Roman Empire in the East, come to terms with the Emperor Zeno, and turned toward Italy. Theodoric the Great, who had been raised as a hostage at the eastern court, defeated Odoacer and set up a powerful Ostrogothic kingdom in Italy.

In Gaul, the successors of Aetius—the military commander Aegidius, Count Paulus, and another military commander named Syagrius—held the region between the Somme and Loire rivers, where they were in contact with the Franks, Alemanni, Burgundians, and Visigoths. These last two peoples were the only ones to found stable kingdoms; the Burgundians set up capitals at Lyons and Geneva, while the headquarters of the Visigoths was at Toulouse.

CLOVIS, KING OF THE FRANKS

One of the Frankish kings of northern Gaul, Childeric, was succeeded by his son Clovis in 482. Clovis first unified the Salian Franks and then overthrew the "Roman kingdom" of Syagrius in 486. In a series of military campaigns, he subjugated the Franks on the Rhine and the Alemanni, thus extending the frontiers of his kingdom to the middle Rhine. In 507, a victory over the Visigoths near Poitiers made Clovis master of the regions of Gaul south of the Loire. Strengthened by his position as a Gallo-Roman aristocrat, and by the support of the Catholic Church (which he enjoyed after his baptism at Rheims), Clovis was recognized by Anastasius, the eastern Roman emperor, as the official heir to the ancient Roman Empire in the West. As king of all the Frankish tribes, Clovis made Paris his capital, and solidly established the Merovingian dynasty (from the name of Meroveus, his legendary ancestor).

Throne of the king Dagobert (628–639). The lower part of the throne, in gilded bronze, imitates chairs of the ancient world. The back and arm rests were added later, in the late 800s. (Collection of Medals, Bibliothèque Nationale, Paris)

PEOPLES WITH A TURBULENT HISTORY

After their defeat by Clovis, the Visigoths moved their kingdom to Spain, with Toledo as their capital. There they confronted the Suevi, just as they had once confronted the Romans in the east. They also retained part of Gaul—the shore from Languedoc to Roussillon, called Septimania.

In England, the Anglo-Saxons remained divided into several rival kingdoms. The most important were those of Kent, Mercia, Northumberland, and Wessex.

Other barbarian peoples remained outside the limits of the western Roman Empire. Some never grew large enough to form states. This was especially true of the Saxons who remained in northern Germany, of the Bavarians, and of the Alemanni, who in 535 accepted the protection of the Franks. Some Germanic groups, however, formed powerful kingdoms. They included the Thuringians between the Elbe and the Weser, beginning in the late 400s; and the Lombards in Hungary, at the beginning of the sixth century. A few decades later, the Lombards, threatened by the westward migration of the nomadic Avars, decided to abandon their kingdom after their neighbors, the Gepids, were crushed by the invaders in 567. Under the leadership of their king, Alboin (who died in 572), the Lombards moved into Italy. (It had been in the hands of the Byzantines since the elimination of the Ostrogoths in 555.) The Lombards seized northern Italy, where they laid the foundations of a powerful kingdom.

THE FATE OF THE BARBARIAN KINGDOMS

Born of the Great Invasions, the barbarian kingdoms of the West had very different destinies. Some lasted only a brief time. The Vandal kingdom of North Africa fell in 533 to a Byzantine reconquest after little more than a century of existence. The Burgundian kingdom was seized by the sons of Clovis in 534, less than a century after its foundation. The realm of the Ostrogoths fell to the Byzantines in 555 after 66 years of existence. The Thuringian kingdom became a Frankish protectorate after 530.

Other kingdoms enjoyed a longer history. That of the Suevi in Spain lasted for nearly two centuries before being annexed in 585 by the powerful Visigoths. The latter, after ruling a century in Aquitaine and then two centuries in Spain, fell in turn to the Arabs in 711. The Lombard kingdom in Italy lasted for two centuries before being conquered by Charlemagne in 774. Some twenty years later, the Avars also fell to Charlemagne.

Some barbarian kingdoms contributed to the building of European states in the Middle Ages. This was the case with the Anglo-Saxons in the ninth century; after three centuries of warfare, Wessex united a number of kingdoms, preparing the way for the birth of medieval England. This was also the case with the Franks.

Alone of the barbarian peoples, the Franks were able to bring about a complete assimilation, thus creating a durable Romano-German civilization from which France was born. The genius of Clovis, who took over intact the administrative department of the "Roman kingdom" in Gaul, explains the astonishing success of this Germanic minority, whose kingdom lasted an astonishing five centuries.

FROM THE MEROVINGIANS TO THE CAROLINGIANS

According to Frankish custom, all male heirs divided the possessions of their father equally when he died. In spite of the territorial divisions that resulted, the Frankish kingdom maintained itself for several centuries by conserving a sense of unity. Reunified for many years by Clotaire II (from 613 to 629) and Dagobert (from 629 to 639), the Frankish kingdom then fell into a long period of anarchy, as the Neustrians northwest of Gaul struggled against the Austrasians east of Gaul. The Austrasians finally prevailed in 687. The Austrasian family of the Pepins played an increasingly important political role: Pepin of Landin, Pepin of Heristal, Charles Martel, and finally Pepin the Short. In 751 Pepin the Short deposed Childeric III, the last of the Merovingians, and had himself elected king in Childeric's place. This event marked the beginning of the Carolingian dynasty. Pepin's coup enabled the Frankish kingdom not only to survive, but to transform itself, fifty years later, into the Frankish empire of Charlemagne.

Gaul and neighboring countries at the time of Dagobert (629–639)

Gaul at the time of Dagobert
Anglo-Saxon Kingdoms
Lombard Kingdoms
Visigothic Kingdoms

The End of an Empire

On the eve of the Great Invasions, the Roman Empire seemed to be as solid as ever. At first centered on the Mediterranean, it had expanded until, by the fourth century, it extended from Britain in the west to Asia Minor in the east, and from the banks of the Rhine and the Danube in the north to North Africa in the south.

Attracted by the wealth of the Roman Empire, barbarians constantly threatened its frontiers, which they had already crossed in the third century. But Rome resisted, and powerful emperors like Diocletian (284–305) and Constantine (306–337) took measures to protect Rome's territories. Reorganized under their rule, the empire became a veritable fortress. Military camps were reconstructed on the frontiers, and cities were protected by strong ramparts. In the countryside, fortifications multiplied. Some barbarian tribes made treaties with Rome. Settled on uncultivated lands near the frontiers, they were responsible for tilling and defending those lands.

In spite of its brilliant civilization, however, the em-

pire showed grave signs of weakness during the fourth century. In the West, increasing administrative and military expenses forced the government to raise taxes to higher and higher levels. To escape these taxes, rich owners left the cities to live on their estates. This trend aggravated social inequalities and provoked many revolts among the people.

The immense size of the empire made it increasingly difficult to govern. In 395 it was divided in two. Constantinople, formerly called Byzantium, became the capital of the Roman Empire in the East, which lasted, as the Byzantine Empire, until 1453. The Roman Empire in the West kept Rome for its capital, although the emperors preferred to live at Trier, Milan, or Ravenna. But the days of the Roman Empire in the West were numbered: in 410 the Visigoths, under the leadership of their king, Alaric, captured Rome.

The heat is overpowering during these last days of August, 410. For several hours the Visigoths have been methodically pillaging Rome. In the Forum, they have assembled their plunder and piled it on their wagons. The inhabitants who were not able to flee or take refuge in the churches are led away into slavery.

A band of starving peasants and rebellious slaves called *bagauds* ("valiant ones" in Celtic), has just attacked a rich Gallo-Roman villa in Aquitaine. Foreseeing that this might happen, the owner of the estate has recruited mercenary soldiers. The experienced soldiers have no trouble repelling the poorly armed and disorganized assailants.

From the ramparts of the fortifications at Mont-Vireux, in the Ardennes, soldiers keep watch over trading vessels on the Meuse River. These auxiliary warriors, Germanic in origin, have been recruited by the Roman authorities because Roman military forces are too few in this troubled time.

At Le Mans, workmen finish building a strong rampart of bricks and stones with a number of semicircular towers. The materials are hoisted by derricks. The city will henceforth be able to resist the coming assaults of the barbarians.

Around 330, the Roman Emperor Constantine and his commanding general inspect the military camp at Drobeta. Established on the banks of the Danube in what is now Rumania, this powerful fortress has just been reconstructed after being abandoned to the barbarians for sixty years. The bridge, built on twenty piers of stone and brick, has also been restored to service. Situated at the mouth of the pass called the "Iron Gates," the bridge had been destroyed to prevent the barbarians from crossing over to the Roman bank of the river in what is today Yugoslavia.

Peoples on the March

Of all the barbarian peoples who were neighbors of the Roman Empire, the Germans were always the most threatening. Since the end of the Roman Republic, they had continually attacked the frontiers of the Rhine and the Danube. Although their murderous raids were always repulsed, they sometimes caused much damage.

During the fourth century, the Germanic world was relatively calm. Feeling less threatened, the Romans became accustomed to the barbarians, hiring them as mercenaries and accepting entire tribes as allies. Economic and even cultural ties linked these peoples that were so different from one another.

Still, the balance was unstable, and it was completely upset by the arrival of the Huns. These Asiatic nomads, attracted by the wealth of the West, invaded Europe in 370. Excellent horsemen who were adept with the sword, the bow, and the lasso, they easily defeated the sedentary Germans.

Directly or indirectly, the Huns caused the flight of entire Germanic peoples across Europe. Some moved vast distances in successive waves. The Visigoths left southern Russia for Gaul, then Spain. Alani, Suevi, and Vandals left central Europe for Gaul; some reached Spain, then went on to North Africa. Other peoples did not journey so far. From Germany, the Franks, Burgundians, and Alemanni moved into northern and eastern Gaul. The Angles, Saxons, and Jutes crossed the North Sea to settle in Britain.

After their migrations, all these people set up kingdoms. Some lasted but a brief time. Others survived longer. And a few gave birth to modern states; this was the case with the Frankish and Anglo-Saxon kingdoms.

The Rhine is frozen. The exceptional cold of the winter of 406 temporarily deprived the Roman Empire in the West of its most precious natural frontier. Taking advantage of the situation, hordes of Vandals, Suevi, Alani, and Burgundians cross the river on December 31, taking care to bypass the fortified city of Mainz, whose military garrison defends the bridge on the Rhine.

It is the month of May in 429, and the little seaport of Tarifa, on a headland in southern Spain, is the scene of unusual excitement. In great disorder, 80,000 Vandals are embarking for North Africa and its wealth. They have requisitioned all available boats. The warriors and their families gather their belongings and the plunder (including horses) already accumulated in Gaul and Spain. Their journey is uncomfortable, but the weather is fine and the voyage across the Strait of Gibraltar takes only a short time.

In April 568, a long procession of people and wagons, escorted by a number of warriors, wends its way across the Hungarian plain. At its head rides Alboin, king of the Lombards, accompanied by his standardbearer. The horizon is on fire, for the people set fire to their fields and villages before leaving. They preferred to destroy their settlements rather than leave them to their old allies, the Avars, who have now become a threat. The Lombards are on their way to Italy, whose fertile lands are poorly defended by the Byzantine army.

The ambassador from Byzantium is received by Attila in 448. A witness of this meeting, the Greek writer Priscus (far right), has left a detailed account of it. The royal palace is located in the heart of the Hungarian plain. Built completely of wood, it is decorated with woolen carpets and luxurious fabrics. The king of the Huns, unlike the nobles around him, is plainly dressed, but he carries weapons and wears a belt studded with gold and precious stones. The favorite wife of the king, attended by a Greek lady-in-waiting, takes part in the interview.

Law and Order

The rise of the Barbarian kingdoms put an end to the anarchy resulting from the Great Invasions. Order was restored, even though it was different from that of the Old Roman Empire in the West. Barbarian kings, originally war leaders elected by their warriors, soon became hereditary sovereigns who wielded absolute power.

The "palace" was the center of barbarian government. Here were to be found the highest officials; these included the chief official (called the mayor of the palace), the constable, and the seneschal. At first fixed in the capital of the kingdom, the palace, like the court, gradually became itinerant—that is, it was to be found wherever the king was staying at the time. Administration and diplomacy required many official documents, which were prepared in palace offices by scribes and notaries directed by the chief clerks. Counts represented the king in the provinces. They exercised all governmental functions—administrative, legal, fiscal, and military. The public treasury was essentially the same as the personal wealth of the king. Gradually, it became more and more difficult to collect direct taxes.

Royal funds came mainly from the revenue of the royal estates, from the spoils of war, from tribute imposed on subjugated peoples, from the coinage of money, from legal fines, and from various tolls and imports.

Although they used Roman law for a time, the barbarians gradually imposed Germanic law. The barbarian tribunal was made up of the free men of the region. It was not up to the accusers to prove the guilt of the accused, but up to the accused to prove his innocence. A barbarian found guilty, was rarely subjected to corporal punishment. Instead, he and his family were generally sentenced to pay some form of compensation, which was divided between the king and the victim or his family.

The tribunal *(mallus)* is sitting because a murder has been committed in the village. A young relative of the victim, backed by his family, loudly accuses a man whose reputation is poor. The accused, upheld by his relatives, tries to prove his innocence. The count of the area and a village leader serve as judges.

In order to prove his innocence, a man has decided to undergo the ordeal—in this case, ordeal by fire. Confronting his accusers, he lifts from a brazier burning charcoal, which he will place on his naked chest. If his burns heal quickly, he will be declared innocent.

In the royal palace, there is intense activity in the office of the scribes. They are preparing administrative documents necessary to govern the kingdom. A clerk, at right, is carefully recopying on parchment an act set down on papyrus and stamped with the royal seal.

A riot rages at Limoges, where the chief clerk, Marcus (far right), has come to collect a tax. The mob is burning the account books and attempting to manhandle the terrified tax collector. Attracted by the shouting, the bishop has come to the defense of poor Marcus and succeeds in calming the rioters. The bishop is more master of the city than the count of Limoges, who is theoretically responsible for law and order.

It is the year 561, and Caribert, Gontran, Childeric, and Sigebert look grave. Their father, King Clotaire, is dead. According to Frankish custom, the four brothers must divide the kingdom as if it were a family inheritance. In order to avoid lengthy discussions, the regions of the kingdom are parceled out among the brothers according to the luck of the draw. Once more (and for many years to come) the kingdom of Clovis has lost its territorial unity.

A Society of Warriors

During the Roman period, wars were fought by permanent armies composed of professional soldiers. This was no longer the case in the barbarian kingdoms; with the Great Invasions spread new, Germanic methods of warfare. The barbarian king was above all a war leader. For him and for his soldiers, war was a sport, dangerous and exhilarating, but also a way to gain riches through plunder. War was also a necessity when a group had to defend itself against threatening enemies or annex new territories in order to survive.

Except for his personal guard made up of professional soldiers, the barbarian king did not have a regular army. When he decided to go to war—in the spring, for no battles took place in the winter—he used his counts to summon most or all of the free men in his realm. His soldiers had to equip themselves at their own expense and furnish supplies for the duration of the campaign.

This method of recruiting soldiers had its drawbacks, for many free men lacked an income large enough to pay for satisfactory war equipment. Thus, the kings were often forced to summon only the rich. They in turn recruited a body of soldiers and provided for their equipment and supplies, either by direct payment or through revenues from lands assigned to them.

In this way mutual bonds, both personal and military, were gradually created between free men and their powerful leaders. These were the origins of the links between nobles and vassals that characterized the feudal society of the Middle Ages.

The Anglo-Saxon king, Redwald, formally presents a ceremonial sword to an allied noble. Its pommel is decorated with two silver rings linked together. Henceforth this will be the symbol of their military alliance. Wearing his helmet, in the form of a human mask, and clothed in the traditional Saxon robe, Redwald holds a heavy royal scepter, the base of which rests on his left knee. His emblem, made of iron, is planted in the earth at his right. At his left stands a young squire, holding the king's battle-ax and shield.

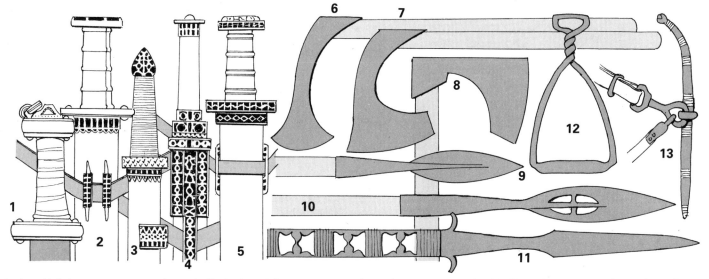

Barbarian chieftains wore ornamental swords (2–5) whose hilts and scabbards were decorated with gold leaf and inlaid garnets. Other, less luxurious swords (1) had a pommel with rings and a silver handguard. Hurling axes, or *francisques* (6), and battle-axes (7,8) were favorite weapons of the Franks. Lance heads (9–11) had various forms; they were sometimes per-

forated among the Lombards of Italy (10), as were the sockets of some hooked lances among the Alemanni (11). Under the influence of nomadic peoples, stirrups (12) were introduced to the West during the seventh century. The horse's bit (13) was carefully ornamented; the prongs of this Alemannic bit are in damascened iron.

Although true military uniforms did not exist, the armies of the various barbarian kingdoms wore battle dress that was quite distinctive, depending on the peoples and the time. Asiatic nomads, the Huns (1) and the Avars (2,3) were remarkable horsemen. The bow was their preferred weapon: they were the only fighters of this period who shot arrows from horseback. Goths (4), Alemanni (5), Lombards (6), and Franks (7) were above all foot

soldiers, even though they moved from place to place on horseback. In general, only the chieftains were protected by defensive armor—helmet, round shield, and, occasionally, breastplate covered with iron plates. Offensive arms were the long sword, the short saber with a single edge, or scramasax (5–7) the battle-ax, and the lance. The barbed spear of the Franks, a kind of iron javelin (7), was more a symbol of command than a hurling weapon.

Hun horseman, fifth century

Avar horse, seventh century

Lombard warrior, seventh century

Frank warrior, about 500 A.D.

Avar Horseman, seventh century

Goth warrior, fifth century

Alemanni warrior, seventh century

Weapons and Battle Tactics

Weapons varied according to periods, peoples, and the social rank of the warriors. Those of the Franks, Alemanni, Lombards, Saxons, and Anglo-Saxons are the best known, since all of these peoples buried a warrior's weapons along with his body.

Offensive weapons consisted of the battle-ax, the lance, the long sword, the saber, and the bow. The Franks in particular fought mainly with battle-axes, at least until about 600. Lances took a great many forms: heavy pikes for foot soldiers, lighter lances for the cavalry, javelins, and so on. Closely related to the Roman *pilum,* the barbed spear was a throwing weapon of the Franks; its blade, as long as its wooden haft, ended in a harpoon point. The long sword, which had a double edge and a damascened blade *(spatha)* was used as much by the cavalry as by foot soldiers. The scramasax, a heavy saber with a single edge, became the favorite weapon of the seventh century. As for the bow, it was the preferred weapon of horsemen like the Huns and the Avars.

Defensive armaments, rare among the barbarians,

were used mainly by their leaders. They included iron helmets decorated with bronze, breastplates covered with iron scales (introduced from the East), and round wooden shields with an iron knob *(umbo)* at the center and sometimes ornamented with bronze.

During the barbarian epoch, the siege techniques of antiquity did not disappear. People still knew how to use them, and built assault machines, such as battering rams. Pitched battles were exceptional, however. More often there were skirmishes or sudden surprise raids. Until the sixth century, battles consisted of confused hand-to-hand fighting, with a welter of individual combats. Later, when warfare began to involve large-scale maneuvers, armaments became more regularized and uniform among some peoples. Only the Goths, Lombards, Alemanni, and Vandals made use of a true light cavalry.

Around 430, a battle rages between Huns and Burgundians. Not far from Worms, on the right bank of the Rhine, the Burgundian rearguard has been surprised by the Hunnish cavalry, which charges down without mercy. After launching a shower of arrows, the Huns attack the Burgundians with whips and lassos. The Burgundian king, Guntar, is killed.

18

Throwing the *francisque,* the formidable battle-ax of the Franks, was a difficult art that required long practice before it could be mastered. Once launched, the weapon turned over and over in the air; the blade could not strike a target except at a precise distance for each battle-ax. In combat, the warrior had to make a quick estimate of the distance in order to hit his target.

Under the expert critical eye of the bailiffs, the best horsemen of the estate put on a display of dressage, obedience trials for the king's show and war horses. This royal stud farm, located near Tours, was one of the most famous in the Merovingian kingdom.

In 539, a Frankish army crosses the Alps and invades Italy. At its head ride Dukes Butilin and Leuthari, whom the Merovingian king, Theodebert, has ordered to make war against the Byzantine general, Narses. The column of Frankish foot soldiers is reinforced by leaders mounted on horses.

Priest, Monks, and Missionaries

At the time of the Great Invasions, Christianity was established mainly in the cities. In almost every case, the city served as the headquarters of a diocese. In its cathedral, the bishop and other clergy celebrated the rituals and dispensed the sacraments of the church (baptism, the eucharist, and so on). Most of the countryside remained pagan. By degrees, however, Christianity spread there, and churches were built in the most important towns *(vici)*.

While certain peoples remained, throughout the barbarian period, believing in a number of gods, others—among them the Goths, Burgundians, Lombards, and Vandals—had already been converted to Christianity. They were not, however, subject to the authority of the pope, for they had accepted Arianism. This heretical doctrine, expounded by a priest named Arius about 300, denied the divinity of Christ.

From the beginning the barbarian kingdoms were treated by the church as missionary lands. The spectacular conversion of princes by great bishops, such as that of Clovis by Saint Remigius of Rheims, sometimes led to the conversion of an entire people, whether pagan or arian. By the eighth century, all the kingdoms had adopted the Christian religion. Nevertheless, many practicing pagans remained in the most isolated areas, a fact that the bishops condemned at the regularly assembled councils.

Monasteries, founded by the hundreds, played a vital role in Christianization. Many of them owed their existence to Irish monks like Saint Gall or Saint Columban. Dividing their time between prayer, study, and manual labor, the monks brought about conversions through their example and the help they gave rural populations.

Shivering, his feet bare and his beard frozen, Saint Walfroy spends long hours every day on top of a column, which he erected on a hill in the Ardennes, near an ancient statue of the goddess Diana. This was the method adopted by this Lombard missionary to turn the pagans away from idol-worship.

The bloodstained bodies of Saint Boniface and his companions lie on a beach along the shore of the North Sea. Their camp was attacked by a band of Frisians, a Germanic people whom the missionaries had courageously undertaken to convert.

Before the Northumbrian court assembled in the palace, two orators confront one another. At the left is a great pagan preacher, and at the right a missionary named Paulin. King Edwin has promised that the victor in this strange duel will decide the religion of his people. Paulin, by common consent, is judged the winner.

The convent of Nivelles, in Belgium, is in mourning because a nun has died. After the funeral ceremony, the procession moves toward the Church of Saint Peter (at the right), where the nuns are buried. The body of the deceased, enveloped in a shroud, is carried on a litter. The convent has two other churches, as was the custom then: Notre Dame, the principal church of the sisters (in the middle) and Saint Paul (at the left), reserved for the priests serving the monastery and the faithful of the area.

An important ceremony is underway in the cathedral of Orleans. In this year of 511, a council has been assembled by the bishops of Gaul and the court. The Arian clergy of old Visigothic Aquitaine, conquered in 507, must solemnly renounce their heresy. Prostrate, the members of the clergy beg for forgiveness and proclaim their loyalty to Catholicism, the religion of the Frankish kingdom since the baptism of Clovis.

Troubles of the Time

"Since every day things go from bad to worse, it is clear that the end of the world is at hand." This inscription can be read at Poitiers on the tomb of the abbott Mellebaude, who died in the seventh century. Like so many of his contemporaries, Mellebaude was struck by the misfortunes of his time. And, like them, he saw in these evils the imminent arrival of the end of the world!

From today's vantage point, the barbarian kingdoms do not seem to have suffered scourges any more numerous or worse than those of antiquity and the later Middle Ages. Natural catastrophes, however, did have dramatic consequences for peoples that relied on agriculture for their livelihood. Floods, violent hailstorms, and prolonged frost or drought lasting several weeks damaged or even ruined future harvests. Sudden invasions of locusts or cattle diseases were just as disastrous. Each emergency led to scarcity or famine, for reserves were small and there was little or no commerce in foodstuffs. At such times families sometimes abandoned children whom they could no longer feed.

Sickness and death were part of daily life for people who were often hungry and totally ignorant of the rules of hygiene. The youngest and the oldest were the first to be stricken. The worst afflictions were the epidemics of contagious diseases, such as dysentery and smallpox, that depopulated whole regions.

Violence, too, was commonplace. Mutilation and murder were resorted to for the most trivial offenses, even within churches. The aristocracy provided an example of endless family feuds. Wars were incessant. Sometimes they pitted entire peoples against each other, but more often they were civil wars, as in Merovingian Gaul.

Besieged for two weeks, the city of Comminges valiantly resists the army of King Gontran. Duke Leudegisele, on horseback at right, encourages his troops. Soldiers use heavy battering rams, mounted on wheels and covered with boards, to try and break down one of the city gates. From the top of the ramparts, the inhabitants hurl stones and pour down burning pitch and boiling oil.

Leaning over the chancel (the sculptured stone balustrade separating the clergy from the faithful) a priest announces that a newborn baby has been abandoned at the church door. A couple appears and agrees to rear the child. If the child is not claimed within ten days, it becomes the slave of the adopting family.

In this night of the year 585, the Ile de la Cité in Paris is burning. The fire, which began not far from the Petit-Pont, spread so rapidly to the opposite bank of the Seine that nothing could stop it. Everything will be destroyed except the cathedral of Saint Etienne and churches built of stone.

The harvest was poor and the stores have been used up. Famine has reigned for many months. In the forest, a man scratches the soil to find some roots that will give his family some meager nourishment.

Pretextat, bishop of Rouen, has dropped his cross and slumped in his seat. Before the horrified gaze of his clergy, a man has stabbed him to death during Easter services. The murderer escapes into the cathedral without anyone attempting to stop him.

A section of the mountain has suddenly become a landslide, burying the fort at Tauredunum, in Switzerland, and blocking the narrow valley of the Rhone. The river has overflowed and carried away entire villages. Some of the inhabitants have lost their lives. Cattle have been drowned, and the harvests are ruined.

Magical Beliefs and Practices

While the faith of new converts to Christianity was vigorous and sincere, the old beliefs survived more or less openly. In order to impose its own authority, the church both attacked beliefs of which it disapproved and accepted ancient practices that were too firmly established to be rooted out.

In the countryside, peasants still venerated the sacred places: springs, groves, mountains, or menhirs. Little by little Christianity, through the efforts of priests, monks, and missionaries, took over such places, which then became the goal of pilgrimages. But in many areas people still celebrated pagan rites that continued those of antiquity, rites based on solstices, eclipses, and the times of planting and harvesting. The church tried to Christianize these celebrations gradually by substituting Christian rites for pagan.

The art of foretelling the future was still very popular. The church condemned it when it was practiced by soothsayers—but reserved the right to ask the saints about the future through prayers and sacred books! The church particularly feared and fought against magical practices, which it believed put people in a danger of losing their souls. It strenuously condemned anyone suspected of commerce with the Devil—fortunetellers, others who cast lots to predict the future, and witches—all of whom it consigned to torture and execution.

Clearly, Christianity was strongly affected by pagan survivals, some of which continued for centuries, Funeral customs are especially revealing: objects buried with the dead, offerings of food, offerings of money, and family meals shared at the tombs. Relics of the saints, sometimes worn simply as amulets, became the objects of growing devotion. They were credited with the power of healing, which extended to the entire tomb of a saint or even to water flowing nearby.

It is festival time at Autun! In order to ensure an abundant harvest, the people of the city pull a statue of the goddess Berecynthia through the fields and vineyards. It is placed on a wagon drawn by oxen. The worshipers sing and dance around the statue, and then carouse late into the night.

A worried man secretly consults an old woman who is thought to be able to predict the future. What does she read in the ashes that she stirs gently with her stick?

These three women of Paris have been condemned to be burned alive. Queen Fredegond, the wife of King Childerio, has accused them of sorcery. She holds them responsible for using magic to cause the death of her young son Thierry.

Assembled for three days on the banks of the sacred lake Helarius in Auvergne, the people throw numerous offerings of bread, cheese, beeswax, and rich fabrics into the water. They also sacrifice animals.

Not far from Benevento in Italy, these Lombard horsemen follow a custom of their ancestors. Riding at a gallop, each tosses a javelin over his shoulder in an attempt to pierce the hide of an animal hung from a sacred tree. Afterwards they will eat the pieces that have fallen off.

It is often necessary to wait patiently for many hours to reach the tomb of Saint Martin, which stands in the choir of a great church near Tours. The stone sarcophagus has been placed on view on a platform. Guided by the clergy, the pilgrims pass through a wooden barrier, one by one. Each wishes to touch the stone of the sarcophagus or the cloth draped over it to obtain some favor or cure from the saint.

Teaching and Learning

Many children from the general population received the rudiments of an education in parish schools. A priest taught them reading and writing, chiefly the Psalms, which they patiently repeated over and over. Other children were sent by their parents while still quite young to monasteries, which took them completely in charge. Young monks-to-be and little nuns were first taught obedience to the rules, followed by grammar, religion, music, sacred texts, and the liturgy.

Young barbarian boys of the upper class received a very different type of education, based mainly on sports and military exercise. They were taught legendary songs celebrating feats of arms by national heroes, and encouraged to follow their examples. The best pupils became squires of the prince, a position that paved the way for brilliant administrative and military careers.

After the fall of the Roman Empire, schools staffed by masters of grammar and rhetoric disappeared. Classical culture was then reserved for an elite of priests, monks, and aristocrats, although the use of the Latin language became more general. Great families of Roman origin did continue to provide their children with tutors who knew classical literature very well. Under the influence of the church, however, teaching changed. There was less emphasis on training keen minds, more on raising toward God the souls of the pupils through discipline and obedience.

Classical culture, though in disfavor with the church, still retained great prestige. From the sixth century on, the church encouraged the production and distribution of sacred texts, liturgical books, and lives of the saints, which were ceaselessly copied and studied in all the great monasteries of the West.

Each summer the monk Valerius transforms his hermitage in Spain into a school. Many children of the region, sent to him by their parents, spend several weeks here learning to read and write. Wooden tablets covered with wax, on which the pupils write with a pointed instrument, serve as notebooks.

Every day this monk of the abbey of Corbie passes long hours at his writing desk. After tracing on a sheet parchment some letters in the form of fantastic animals, he "illuminates" them—decorates them with bright colors. Nothing is too beautiful to illustrate this copy of a book by Saint Augustine.

Munegasil is trying on a hernia bandage which the doctor says he should wear. This medical apparatus has to fit precisely in order to alleviate his pain. The hernia is compressed by a woven pad covered by a meta! plate that is held tightly in place by a leather belt.

The Roman Emperor in the East, Leo I, is quite pleased to see that young Theodoric, seated beside him, is a very good student. The emperor compliments Theodoric's teacher, Flavius Ardabus Aspar. The education of the prince, a future king of the Ostrogoths (a hostage in Byzantium since the age of eight), is well underway.

Wishing to thank God for having answered a prayer, or simply anxious to provide a religious education, the parents of these young boys have chosen to place them in a monastery. Life is not too hard for these "child monks"; they enjoy pleasant moments of recreation after prayers, study, and religious music.

Family Life

As in the Roman Empire, the head of the family continued to wield absolute authority, including the power of life and death. The existence of each member was governed by the father's decisions, which were in turn dictated by the interests of the family as the basic unit of society.

In pagan families, a newborn baby was named on the eighteenth day after birth. The name was bestowed by the person who carried the baby officially to the bath. Among Christians, baptism was usually delayed until adolescence. Cleansed of original sin and blessed by God, the young Christian thenceforth had a godfather who would replace his father if the latter died before the child reached adulthood.

Childhood was always a very short stage in the life of a young barbarian, who was supposed to become an adult as quickly as possible. Reared by his mother or by a nurse, a boy might watch over the herds or attend school, but always took part in strenuous outdoor sports.

The first coming-of-age for boys was celebrated at fifteen among the Burgundians and Anglo-Saxons,

fourteen among the Visigoths, and twelve among the Franks. This was the age at which a young man was expected to go to war.

Marriage marked the real entrance of a young barbarian into adult society. It was preceded by betrothal, a period of great importance, for the two families had to come to an agreement about the terms of the marriage contract, often at a price that made it seem like a commercial transaction. The feelings of the engaged couple were rarely considered, especially those of girls, who were often quite young at the time. The wedding took place much later. Among Christians, there was a nuptial benediction by a priest, after which the young bride was conducted to the house of her new family.

Under the watchful eyes of their two families, Amalric and Deoteria exchange the traditional kiss, which makes their betrothal official. According to custom, the young man slips a silver ring onto the finger of the young girl. He also gives her jewels, delicacies, and a pair of slippers. He has handed over to his future father-in-law a purse, which symbolizes the purchase of his fiancee.

At the moment of the nuptial benediction, Chrodulf and Childegonthe kneel before the priest and join hands. An altar cloth is held over their heads to ensure that their union will be blessed and their lives happy.

The marriage banquet is over. Escorted by a joyful and noisy procession, the father of Childegonthe takes her in his arms and carries her across the threshold of her new house. As is the custom, the hair of the young married woman is plaited into six braids.

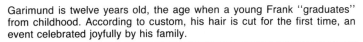

Garimund is twelve years old, the age when a young Frank "graduates" from childhood. According to custom, his hair is cut for the first time, an event celebrated joyfully by his family.

Several adolescents are baptized on Easter Eve. Their godparents have accompanied them to the baptistery. After undressing at the edge of the baptismal pool, the young people immerse themselves in the water three times before the bishop anoints them with holy oil.

Eulalius has decided to rescue his fiancee, Agnechilde, from a convent at Lyons, which her parents forced her to enter. At dawn, the young girl climbs through a window and, with the help of her fiance, slips onto his horse. The two ride off as fast as they can.

How Women Lived

Although women played a very important role as mistresses of households and mothers of families, society and the law imposed oppressive restrictions on them.

A barbarian woman married very young unless she entered a convent. In contrast with Roman times, when divorce by mutual consent was allowed, marriages could hardly ever be dissolved. This stability guaranteed the unity of the family and protected the wife, since her husband could not easily abandon her. Women, however, could not inherit. This meant that, in almost all barbarian kingdoms, landed property and real estate could not be handed down by women; about all they could pass on were a few clothes, jewels, and some objects of common use.

Still, certain women of the barbarian era are known to history. Some were queens of scandalous behavior and legendary violence, like Fredegond and Brunhilda of the Frankish court. Others were wise and clever queens, such as Clotilda or Bathilda, wives of the Frankish kings Clovis I and Clovis II, respectively. Still others were abbesses who were both powerful and feared, among them Bertille of Chelles, Theodechilde of Jouarre, or Radegunda of Poitiers.

Barbarian women attached great importance to their clothes and adornments. Every people had its own feminine fashions, which evolved over the time. A Visigoth or a Lombard, married to a Frank, wore her "national" costume all her life, although she usually added a few items of local fashion. Just as the number of a man's weapons showed his rank in society, so the richness of a woman's clothes and jewels indicated her status.

Inspired by Saint Eligius, whom one of her relatives had seen in a dream, Queen Mother Bathilda, widow of Clovis II, has decided to sell her splendid set of golden jewelry for the benefit of the poor. In the presence of Bertille, abbess of the convent of Chelles, where she has retired, the old sovereign is carefully examining an embroidered linen tunic held up by a young nun.

Women's clothes in the barbarian era differed according to the people and period, as tomb excavations show. Except in the Oriental world (5, 8, 9) dresses and shirts ended just below the knee. The sleeves of coats and jackets were sometimes embroidered in gold (1) or with rows of pearls (6). Stockings were held up by garters (1), and shoes were fastened with metal buckles. Pins (6, 7, 8) and sometimes diadems (5, 8, 9), kept the hair in place; veils were usually worn only by married women. While earrings, necklaces, and rings were purely ornamental, brooches were useful as well as fasteners for dresses, cloaks, and coats. A belt was very important, for a woman usually used it to carry a purse, a knife, keys, a comb, and various good luck charms.

(1) Frankish, about 600; (2) Frankish, beginning of the sixth century; (3) Gothic, fifth century; (4) Visigothic, first half of the sixth century; (5) Slavic, seventh century; (6) Alemannic, about 500; (7) Alemannic woman and little girl, mid-seventh century; (8) Gepid, sixth century; (9) Hunnish, fifth century; (10) Frisian, early fifth century.

Pleasures and Entertainment

The barbarians were quick to take over many of the refinements of Roman civilization. Germanic overlords, often installed in the palaces or luxurious villas of their Roman predecessors, adopted several of their pastimes, such as the traditional games of handball, dice, chess, and backgammon. Many, like the Frankish King Childebert, the Ostrogothic King Theodoric, or the Visigothic Queen Ultrogoth, laid out magnificent pleasure gardens. Children enjoyed traditional pastimes: tops, balls, knucklebones, dolls, animal toys, and so on.

Entertainments were often arranged on the occasion of a religious festival or a fair. People watched plays or mimes and listened to the songs of bards who accompanied themselves on a lyre or a harp. In fact, music and song were among the most popular pleasures. Religious ceremonies, marriages, funerals, the return of a victorious king—all took place to the sound of music. Such events were always an excuse for public merrymaking, too. Those who caroused at banquets enjoyed dancing and tended to get excessively drunk. The church condemned these excesses, often in vain.

Men and boys loved violent sports and outdoor pleasures, especially riding and swimming. In the ancient amphitheaters, which had been restored, big crowds gathered to watch fights between wild beasts.

But the favorite amusement of men throughout the barbarian period was hunting, whether with the net, the falcon, or on horseback. The promise of fresh game was of less appeal than the confrontation with animals and the pleasure of proving one's skill and courage.

Taverns abound in Paris, but few are as famous as Mother Gibethrude's on the Ile de la Cité. She serves wines of such quality that no honey is needed to sweeten them. The owner's meat platters and fried fish from the Seine are much appreciated by the noisy guests.

Boar hunting is a dangerous sport, especially when practiced with a hunting spear. Cornered by beaters and harassed by tireless, growling dogs, the beast has charged the hunter and impaled itself on his firmly held lance.

In the old Barcelona forum, three unemployed men play for hours with black stone pieces. They move them quickly on a board scratched in the flagstones. Nearby, children play in the middle of the esplanade with a leather ball.

The ancient Roman amphitheater at Metz has been more or less restored, and games are being held for King Childebert and his court. In this period combats between gladiators have been replaced by ferocious struggles between animals. Here, before the eyes of fascinated spectators, a bear is attacked by mastiffs.

The most popular meeting place for the young Vandal aristocrats in Carthage is on the hill of Byrsa. Boys and girls spend a lot of time here, talking and joking, far from the eyes of their parents. Often a servant has to be sent out to find them and persuade them to return.

Funeral Rites

Cemeteries were outside of towns and villages, but not far away. Tombs were usually marked above ground by steles (inscribed stones) or by stone enclosures. A hillock of earth, or tumulus, sometimes covered the grave of a pagan chieftain. Some leaders, like the Anglo-Saxon King Redwald (buried at Sutton Hoo about 630), were buried in their boats, according to Norse custom. Graves, often dug on an east-west axis, were usually aligned with one another. Near the towns (and later in the countryside, too), tombs were grouped around and even inside churches. People wanted to lie as close as possible to the tombs or relics of the martyrs and saints above which the churches had been built.

The type of tomb varied according to the people, the era, and the social rank of the deceased. A body might be deposited in the bare earth, in a coffin, or in a funeral chamber built with planks wedged with stones. Sarcophagi were used mainly in the city cemeteries and in regions that had preserved Roman traditions.

The Franks, Alemanni, Lombards, Saxons, and Anglo-Saxons buried their dead clothed in their finest garments along with such personal objects as jewels for the women and weapons for the men. Containers in the tomb were sometimes filled with food. Clearly, the deceased wanted to be surrounded by the insignia of rank, even in the tomb. Other peoples, however—the Goths, the Burgundians, and the Vandals—generally did not follow these customs.

A funeral procession has reached the cemetery near the village. The inhabitants of Morken, in the Rhineland, are giving their chieftain a burial worthy of his rank. The dead man, carried on a litter by his most faithful companions, has been dressed in his best clothes. His shield rests on his body, while his two sons carry his helmet and his sword. The people have dug a large grave and lined it with planks. The Frankish chieftain will be placed in it inside a solid wooden coffin.

The body of a man has been placed on a funeral pyre in the presence of his family. Afterward the ashes will be gathered in a pottery urn and buried in the cemetery. Cremation was not practiced much in this era, except among the northern Germans and in England.

During the Merovingian period, graves were often marked by blocks of stone or carved steles. Sometimes rectangular enclosures surrounded one or two graves. Cemeteries were developed according to a regular plan.

After the funeral ceremonies, workmen carefully lower a heavy stone sarcophagus into the grave they have dug below the floor of the basilica of Saint Denis. In spite of the derrick and pulley, the operation is a delicate one. Later, the men will fill in the grave and replace the stones.

According to a pagan Roman tradition, followed mainly in North Africa and Spain, the family of the deceased gathers around the tomb on the anniversary of his or her death to take part in a funeral meal. The grave, topped by a soberly decorated marble table (the *mensa),* is surrounded by a slop-ing bench on which the guests recline as if for a banquet. While dining, they symbolically offer the dead man or woman a drink, pouring the wine into an opening connected to the tomb below.

The Daily Round

For the most part, the people of the barbarian kingdoms were peasants, who worked hard to wrest a meager living from the land and who lived by the rhythm of the seasons. It was not uncommon in the Germanic countries for people to own a plowshare made of iron and a two-wheeled cart drawn by a pair of oxen. Elsewhere, most farmers continued to use the traditional wooden plow or even just a hoe. Iron tools, such as scythes, sickles, axes, and spades, were relatively scarce and treated with great care. Fertilizing with manure—either domestic or from birds raised for the purpose—went on as earlier. But the chief method of returning fertility to the soil was by letting the land lie fallow. In the northern and eastern regions of Barbarian Europe, a field was usually left unplanted every other year; this meant that in any given year, only half the land was under cultivation.

Grain and beans were the main crops. Harvesting grain required a big work force to wield the sickles. The grain was then beaten with a flail or trampled underfoot by animals. After being dried in the sun, it was ground as needed on the family millstone or at the nearest water mill.

There was some progress in animal breeding, but the livestock of the average peasant consisted mainly of sheep, goats, and pigs. People rarely slaughtered cattle or horses for food; these animals were too precious as beasts of burden or transportation.

Like the Romans, the barbarians, cultivated grape vines and appreciated good vintages. After the harvest, people stored wine in vats or pottery jars, then put it in wooden barrels bound with iron and coated inside with pitch. Beekeeping was very common, for honey was the only sweetener, and the wax provided candles. People also tapped the resources of the sea—salt as well as fish.

Clearing the forest is a hard but necessary task when the community needs more land for cultivation. These peasants have felled several trees and are struggling to uproot the stumps. They are supervised by monks from the neighboring abbey, which owns this thicket.

Autumn has come. It is the season for sowing, before the first snowfall. A farmer leans heavily on the plow, so as to push the plowshare (made of fire-hardened wood) through the earth. The straight beam of this rudimentary plow is fixed to a yoke, which is tied in turn to the horns of two oxen. A second farmer scatters the seed immediately, while a third closes up the furrows with a horse-drawn wooden harrow.

Water from a river, which has been diverted by means of a millrace, is turning the large paddle wheel of a mill. The wheel engages the wooden gears, which turn a heavy stone grinding wheel. A monk counts the bags of wheat that the miller is busily grinding. After the flour collects on the fixed wheel, it is put into sacks.

The fishing has been good. Fishermen from the island of Guennoc, on the north coast of Brittany, are beaching their flat-bottomed boat and unloading baskets overflowing with fish. In the distance, surrounded by a wall, lies their village with its stone walls and thatched roofs. At the right stands a cross—actually a prehistoric standing stone that has been reshaped—for the Bretons are Christians.

Villages and Large Estates

After having invaded the provinces of the ancient Roman Empire of the West, the barbarians settled on the lands they had conquered. They claimed vast domains for themselves, and many formed a new landed elite, becoming neighbors of and joining themselves by marriage to the old Roman aristocracy.

Each king owned huge territories on which he levied taxes. Cultivated and fallow lands, forests, heaths, and moors constituted the royal "fisc," or treasury, which was slowly depleted by successive gifts to the church and the great overlords.

The large rural estate, or *villa,* was composed of two parts: One, the "reserve," consisting of the best land, was worked by the owner with slaves and salaried workers. The other, divided into family farms, was rented to peasants, usually free men, who owed the proprietor part of their crop and certain tasks to be performed on the reserve. Actually, few estates consisted of a single tract; in most cases, lands were split up. Always anxious to increase the size of their estates, great landowners often seized land from free

peasants who asked for their protection or help. More and more of them deserted the cities and visited their estates one after the other, staying in luxurious homes.

The peasants lived in villages of wooden houses that either made up part of the great estates or were independent. The most important among them, the *vici,* had been in existence in the Roman era (as had many of the estates). Situated on the main roads, they served as small country towns, with a market and a church. Taxes were collected there and coins minted.

In the village of Warendorf in Westphalia, each family owns a group of thatched wooden buildings, clustered around a well. The villagers live in large houses with exterior supports (right). Smaller buildings (left) are used as stables, barns, or workshops. Circular granaries with movable roofing (background) protect the fodder.

Having been forced out of their own territory, this family of peasants has arrived at the outskirts of a village. The villagers, assembled behind their chief, study the new arrivals. They will be welcomed if agreement is unanimous, but only at the end of a year will the villagers decide whether they can stay for good.

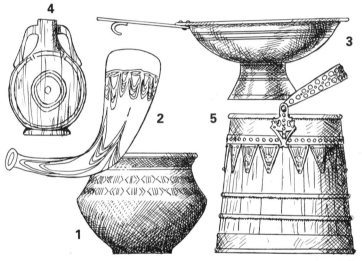

In the barbarian kingdoms, dishes and utensils were many and varied. There were pottery vessels with a few decorations (1), simple glassware (2), and bronze containers (3); the finest of these were imported from the Mediterranean countries. Wooden containers, which were very common, included drinking flasks (4), and buckets with iron and bronze trim (5).

This wooden village house has no partitions, just one large room. A fire is kindled at one side, directly on the ground. This part of the room serves as the kitchen and dining room. Such household activities as weaving take place here, too. The family sleeps in the other half of the room.

A poet named Fortunatus has described for us the estate of Bishop Nicetius of Trier as it was in the sixth century. Situated on a bend of the Moselle River, it is encircled by a long wall guarded with thirty towers. The access bridge is defended by a tower and catapults. The bishop's huge palace lies on top of the hill. On its flanks are terraces of fields, vineyards, and orchards.

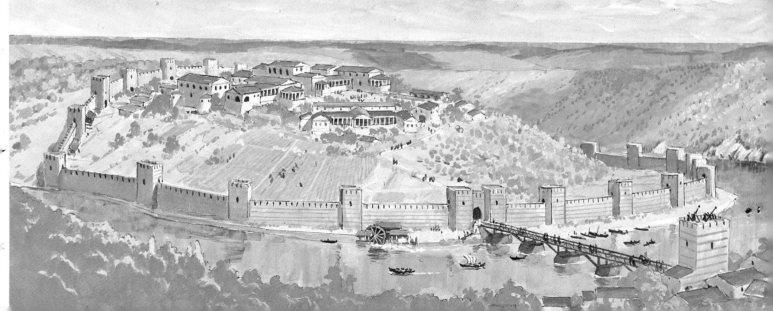

Cities and City Dwellers

During the Great Invasions, most of the cities that had been the pride of the Roman Empire of the West fell into the hands of the barbarians. Although the latter pillaged them, they did not destroy them entirely. On the contrary, many barbarians acquired a taste for urban life. Several kings set an example by choosing ancient Roman cities for their capitals. The Ostrogoth Theodoric installed himself in Ravenna; Alaric, the Visigoth, in Toulouse; the Burgundian Gondebad in Lyons and Geneva; Clovis in Paris; and the Vandal Genseric in Carthage.

Towns that were not used for royal residences saw their administrative importance decline in favor of their religious role, as diocesan headquarters. But they did remain economic centers, enriched by merchants and craftsmen.

In many ways, the cities of the barbarian West differed little from what they had been at the end of the Roman era. They kept their basic plans in the right-angled layout of their streets, as well as their squares, houses, sewers, and walls. Beyond the walls remained the access roads, aqueducts, suburbs, and cemeteries. Many public monuments survived, too. Some, restored and maintained by kings or bishops, kept their original function. This was true of palaces, basilicas, baths, and amphitheaters in Paris, Soissons, Rome, and Ravenna. Other monuments fell into ruin or were adapted for other uses—for instance, law courts were transformed into churches. Outlying districts were sometimes allowed to decay, as at Milan. On the other hand, some districts were renewed with the construction of numerous churches.

On the third floor of an old Gallo-Roman house in Angers, Duke Beppoleno and his friends are celebrating. Suddenly the rotten flooring, covered by terra cotta tiles, collapses without warning. Furniture, dishes, and guests slide into the gaping hole. Beppoleno is yanked back just in time by two of his companions.

Partly abandoned during the Great Invasions, this residential quarter of Milan is newly occupied. Huts have been put up in the grounds of a rich villa, whose marble colonnade is still standing. The villa's former *impluvium* (pool for catching rain) is now used as a drinking pond for animals. The garden has been plowed up. The city has lost its former splendor. In the background an ancient temple still stands, now transformed into a church.

On Easter Eve, the bishop arrives to celebrate baptisms. Preceded by the clergy, a long procession of newly baptized, clothed in white robes, leaves the baptistery. The young people are making their way toward the cathedral to take part in a solemn mass and receive communion for the first time. According to Merovingian custom, the heart of the city was endowed with a second cathedral church (right), with the bishop's palace, as well as with other churches and some monasteries.

Duke Rauching's wife wears a haughty look as she parades in the streets of Soissons, escorted by her guards. Dressed in expensive robes, she wears heavy gold jewelry set with colored stones. Her horse's harness, of fine leather and gilded silver, was a gift from her husband. The noble lady and her squire pass close to the market, which is installed at the foot of the old Gallo-Roman wall.

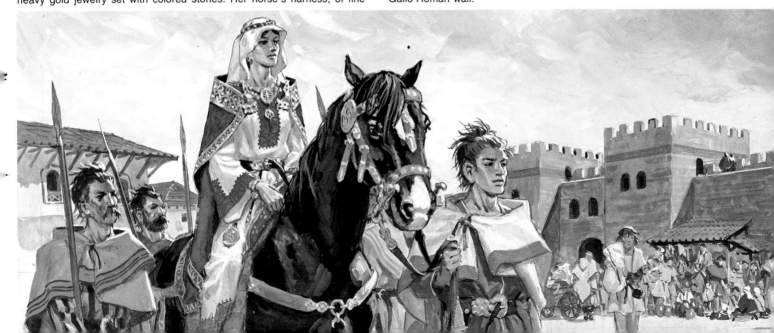

The Artisans' Quarter

As had been the case during the Roman era, artisans learned their specialty with a master and under his authority. For instance, Saint Eligius learned his with the goldsmith and coiner of money, Abbo.

These whose trades did not require much room—goldsmiths, makers of coins, tailors, weavers, furriers, saddlemakers, and the like—had their workshops in the heart of the city, near the traders' shops. Outside the city were the kilns of potters, brickmakers, and tile-makers; the smelters of workers in bronze, silver, and glass; and the workshops of carpenters and workers in bone.

Certain very specialized craftsmen had to stay in one place—workers in mosaic or fresco, for instance, or architects, or the carpenters who repaired wooden water pipes. Other craftsmen traveled from village to village. These included the metalworkers who repaired armor, tools, jewelry, and metal containers. All in all, good craftsmen were scarce, and the best qualified were brought in from a great distance if needed: masons, carpenters, makers of musical instruments, glassmakers, even gardeners, cooks, bakers, and doctors.

Some artisans were free men who plied their trade in cities, towns, and large villages. Others, who were either half-free or slaves, worked for a master. Those who worked in metal or textile production were often grouped in workshops that were usually located on the great lay and church estates.

At Huy, on the banks of the Meuse River, the artisans' quarter is situated at the edge of town. On the left, a potter is making clay vessels on a potter's wheel, which is being turned by his helper. The vessels are fired in ovens. Afterward, the top of the oven is broken so that the vessels can be removed. On the right, a bronze-worker is pumping his bellows vigorously to melt the metal, which has been placed in earthen crucibles. His helper is kneading clay mixed with horse dung to make the two-part molds. Their two halves are stamped with the wooden or metal object to be reproduced in bronze. The molds must dry before being used.

On the right, a goldsmith embosses a little funeral cross that he has cut from a sheet of gold. He stamps a motif and then repeats it with a die made of engraved bronze. On the left, another goldsmith solders filigree onto a brooch. The delicate motifs, in twisted gold wire, are held in place on the surface of the ornament by tallow and tin solder. The necessary heat is obtained from the burning point of a charcoal stick, kept hot by a blowpipe.

A bronze-worker has buried his clay molds so that they will not burst during the pouring. Using a wooden handle, he lifts a crucible from the fire and pours the molten metal into the molds, making showers of sparks.

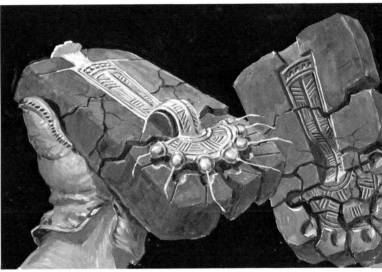

The clay mold is still red-hot when the bronze-worker digs it out. He breaks it apart with a hammer blow, freeing the sparkling bronze brooch. He finishes the ornament by filing off the needle-like threads of metal that have formed at the edge of the mold.

Barbarian jewelry was made using two different techniques. One was that of cloisonné. It consisted of covering the surface to be decorated with soldered compartments; into these were inserted thin pieces of garnet or colored glass (2, 3, 5, 6, 8, 10, 11). In the second technique, individual settings were soldered onto a surface and multicolored stones inserted into them

(1, 4). Solid gold or silver was poured into molds (7), and was often finished off with garnets (9, 12). Some jewelry took the form of animals: eagles (3), heads of birds of prey (12), S-shaped two-headed monsters (5), or fish (8). Human representations were rare and usually showed the face of Christ.

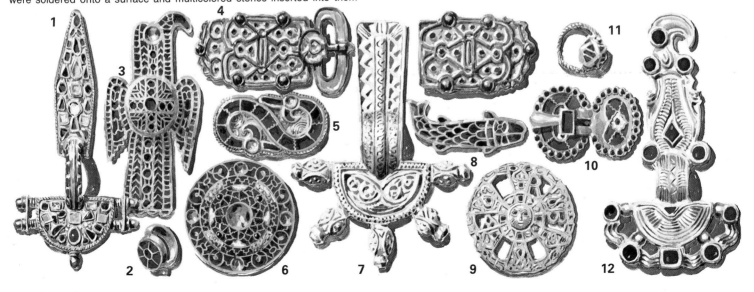

1 3 4 11 5 8 10 2 6 7 9 12

The Art of Metalworking

Of all of the arts that used fire or heat practiced in the barbarian West, the craft of metalworking was the most highly developed. Unlike pottery or glassware, work in welded, embossed, or molded metals—gold, silver, bronze—was always executed with great skill, although according to the fashions and tastes of the time. It was iron ware, however, that reached unequaled perfection. Craftsmen excelled particularly in making damascened steel (which has wavy lines like fine moiré) and other damascened objects, inlaid with threads of silver and brass wire.

Smelters were often located next to mines that had been worked since antiquity—for instance, in the Rhineland and in Lorraine. Forests were indispensable, since smelting the ore into iron required vast quantities of wood. Metal had to be forged for a long time to produce the soft iron or steel ingots needed for making damascened blades. These ingots were sent to forges installed on the outskirts of cities or on the great estates. There the best smiths, jealously guarding the secrets of their art, made fine tools and arms of high quality.

The art of damascening was brought to the West by Eastern craftsmen. (The term comes from the Syrian city of Damascus.) It requires no fixed installations. Along with a set of light tools and a few easily carried materials such as sheets of silver and threads of silver and brass, the damascener had to transport only the pieces of iron already prepared at the forge and ready for decorating—trimmings for belts, accessories for harnesses, and so on.

At this forge, the craftsmen know all the secrets of making swords with damascened blades, famous for their strength and ornamentation. On the right, two workmen use tongs to twist a bar of damascene made of strips of soft iron and steel welded together. On the left, the master smith pounds on the blade of a sword. The rods of damascene and the sword blade have to be reheated frequently in the raised furnace.

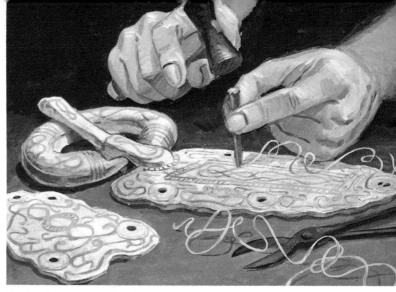

Firmly supported by logs, the gallery of this iron mine is lit by stone lamps filled with grease. The miners are protected by caps and black leather aprons, but have stripped off their shirts because of the heat. After attacking the rock with pickaxes, they will load the ore into wagons.

Much time and skill are necessary to make a sword with a damascene blade. First of all, the smith stacks four bands of pure iron (in white in drawing 1), alternating them with three bands of steel (in black). Then he welds them by pounding them with his hammer into a bar about 1/3 of an inch thick (2). He twists this bar while it is hot (3) before hammering it again into a square section. Then the smith places three bars of damascene side

Having drawn decorative lines on pieces of iron, the damascener is engraving them with a chasing tool. He inserts a thread of copper in the small furrows he has made and hammers it down with a piece of hard wood. Next, he will plate the undecorated areas with a thin sheet of silver.

by side (4) and beats them into the form of a sword blade (5) about 1/6 of an inch thick. He inserts it between steel cutting edges (6) and then welds everything together (7). Finally he polishes the entire blade and dips it in a bath of acid. Only then is the damascened ornamentation revealed, with a light color for the iron and a dark one for the steel.

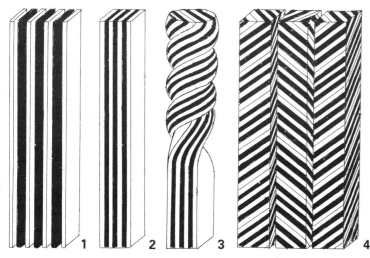

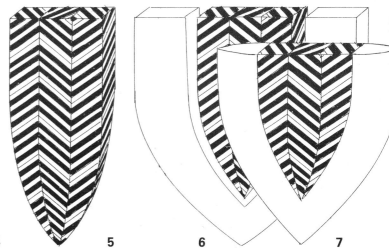

Furnaces constructed of stones and clay have been built into a hill. On the right a kiln is working full blast. Through a top opening workers are shoveling in charcoal and iron ore, alternating the two. At the far right, a helper keeps the fire hot by pumping on a large bellows. Two other bellows, lying

on the ground, were pumped through holes at the base of the kiln to get the fire going. On the left two men pull a ball of glowing metal from another kiln. It must be worked at the forge for a long time before it becomes high quality steel.

Quarries and Construction Sites

Greco-Roman architectural design and techniques remained very much alive in the barbarian kingdoms of Italy, Gaul, Spain, and North Africa. The best evidence of this can be found in the numerous religious monuments erected during this period.

As in late antiquity, walls were constructed in a pattern of "small stones"—that is, of quarried rocks arranged in regular rows. Building exteriors were often decorated with terra cotta. Marble was in great demand for columns, capitals, and chancels, and to finish walls and floors. Although builders frequently reused older marble, they continued to work the best quarries of Italy and the Pyrenees region. Architects usually covered churches with wooden ceilings or, even simpler, built a framework to support the roof. The roof might be made of tiles or of lead or copper sheets. Mosaics and frescoes were often assigned to Byzantine artists from the Roman Empire in the East.

In the less Romanized regions of barbarian Europe—especially England and the northern Germanic lands—as well as in heavily forested areas, wood replaced stone as the basic construction material. It was used for farm buildings, churches, and the luxurious homes of the aristocracy. Barbarian workers were masters of carpentry.

The ancient custom of burying the dead in sarcophagi, a tradition that continued in the barbarian epoch, also stimulated work in the stone and marble quarries. In the Paris area, plaster was substituted for stone to produce molded sarcophagi.

Near the big cemetery surrounding the church of Sainte-Croix-et-Saint-Vincent at Paris, artisans are mass-producing plaster sarcophagi. They mold them using a double framework of boards. After several weeks of drying in a shed, the sarcophagi can be transported and used. In the background, wagons carry gypsum from a nearby quarry. It will be heated on a blazing fire and made into plaster.

Shaped in a wooden mold, flat clay bricks all have the same dimensions. One board of the mold has a carved decoration that serves to ornament one edge of each brick. After drying, the bricks and tiles are baked in kilns.

In a marble quarry in the Pyrenees, a stone mason carves a capital in the Corinthian style. Behind him are quarrymen at work. As they cut blocks of marble from alternate layers, the face of the wall takes on the appearance of a staircase.

Quarrymen of Arcy-sur-Cure, mounted on a scaffold, wield pickaxes to shape a trapezoidal block of limestone out of which a sarcophagus will be hollowed. In order to detach masses of stone from the face of the quarry, the men use wooden wedges doused with water to make them expand. An inclined plane will enable them to slide the block down to the stonecutter.

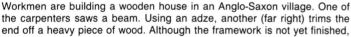

Workmen are building a wooden house in an Anglo-Saxon village. One of the carpenters saws a beam. Using an adze, another (far right) trims the end off a heavy piece of wood. Although the framework is not yet finished, other workers are beginning to lay the floor and raise the walls made of split logs. They will cover the roof with thatch.

Merchants and Shopkeepers

Although commerce still thrived in the cities, it slowed down considerably in the countryside. The great estates tended to be self-sufficient, and sold only a meager surplus of their grain, vegetables, fruit, wine, honey, and game to neighboring towns and villages.

By contrast, there was a busy long-distance trade in luxury goods. It was dominated by Eastern merchants, who dealt in a number of expensive products: exotic fruits, fine cloth, perfume, jewels, precious metals, and so on. They had little trouble finding buyers among the wealthy thousands who formed their clientele: kings and their courts, the great landowners, the upper clergy, and monasteries.

As soon as valuable merchandise was unloaded, it was placed in the *cellarius* of the port, a sort of customs building where excise officials levied import duties. Then it was distributed to the shopkeepers of the town and to the traveling merchants who visited the palaces and the European fairs, including those at Saint Denis, Arles, Cologne, and Pavia.

The traffic in slaves was just as profitable. Supplied mostly by England and the northern countries, it provided manpower for the great estates.

Gold became scarce. Barbarian kings did not control the currency supply. Instead it was in the hands of specialized craftsmen, the coiners of money, who might also be goldsmiths. In any case, less and less money circulated. The greed of the rich, who reinvested little of their wealth, was one of the chief causes of the economic stagnation of the barbarian kingdoms.

The fair at Saint Denis has been in full swing for several days now. It is organized every year by the monks from the abbey in order to sell their wine and honey. Sitting on a barrel (at left), a buyer tastes the wine and negotiates his price. Many traveling merchants stroll through the crowd.

On a quay at the port of Ostia, a merchant shows a young Berber slave girl to a possible buyer. Like her companions, she has been captured in North Africa and brought by boat to Italy, where there is a ready market for all sorts of household and field workers.

After long bargaining, a trapper and a merchant have agreed on the price of a bundle of furs. Watched attentively by the seller, the buyer uses a small scale to weigh the coins corresponding to the sum agreed upon in order to make sure of their value.

Having placed a disk of gold on the fixed metal die (the reverse), the minter puts a movable die (the face) on top of it and then gives a mighty blow with his hammer. In this way, he stamps both sides of the coin with the designs engraved on the dies. His helper is molding small ingots of gold.

The Eastern merchants' quarter of Marseilles is always very lively. In the narrow streets overlooking the port, the shops of Greek, Jewish, and Syrian traders overflow with varied merchandise brought by ship from Asia and Africa—valuable cloth, purple-dyed leather, rare furs, colored jewels, rolls of papyrus, and glass vials filled with aromatic perfume. Foodstuffs include jars of olive oil, jugs of Byzantine wine, spices, dates, and figs.

On Roads and Rivers

The basic arteries of the network of roads the Romans had built in the West still existed. But the infrastructure, which had contributed much to the prosperity of the Empire, had fallen into disrepair. Many stone bridges had disappeared, to be replaced by less sturdy wooden structures, by bridges made of boats, or by ferries. Many waterways were crossed simply by fording. The poorly kept roads could not withstand the effects of bad weather. Thus, communication was considerably slowed down. Though some horsemen could still ride 25 to 45 miles a day, vehicles could cover barely 20 miles. Travelers were often stopped when frontiers were closed, or subjected to compulsory searches carried out by agents of the various kings. The sovereigns levied taxes on merchandise, but failed to use these funds to keep up the roads.

Only servants of the state, provided with official documents authorizing them to carry out requisitions, benefited from the relative comfort of the royal relays and could find wagons in good repair and fresh horses. All other travelers—small traders, pilgrims, or private individuals—traveled at their own risk unless accompanied by an escort to protect them from robbers. The wealthy traveled in comfortable carriages. Many used four-wheeled or two-wheeled wagons drawn by horses.

The hazards of overland routes encouraged the use of river transport. Passengers and merchandise were carried on long, narrow barges that plied the Rhine, the Moselle, the Seine, and the Rhone.

The old Roman road is badly kept, and traffic has a difficult time in winter. The heavy oxcart (*carruca*) of a troop of actors is stuck in deep, muddy ruts. Carelessly speeding by is a light vehicle drawn by four horses (*rheda*). Two clerics on horseback, unable to pull back in time, are splattered with mud.

The sanctuary of the Egyptian martyr Saint Mena, at Karm-Abu-Mina, is seen in the distance. Here at last is the end of a long journey for these Frankish pilgrims. First they had to get to Marseilles. After crossing the Mediterranean to Alexandria, they finally walked for several days across the desert.

King Gontran wants to maintain order in his kingdom of Burgundy. He has stationed armed men at the frontiers to guard the road closely. They search travelers and their baggage, not sparing members of the clergy. Some merchandise is subject to taxation.

Floating down the Rhone, this flat-bottomed boat approaches the city of Arles. To let it through, a bridge of boats used to cross the river has been opened at the middle, with the help of the current. As soon as the boat passes, the bridge will be closed as horses on either side of the river pull back on ropes.

A strange caravan wends its way along the banks of the Garonne River. To carry his luggage and booty seized by his army, Gondovald has used, not horses or mules, but camels. Brought by ship from North Africa, these strange animals astonish the inhabitants, but prove to be very useful beasts of burden.

At Sea

After the Great Invasions, the seas were traveled as much as they had been at the end of the Roman epoch. In spite of pirates and shipwrecks, journeys by water were safer than those by land.

The Mediterranean was crisscrossed by trading ships that sailed along the coasts or maintained a permanent connection between East and West by transporting goods and passengers. The traders—Greeks, Egyptians, Jews, and Syrians—who often hired ships from owners in Alexandria, formed convoys escorted by the Byzantine navy. Their holds carried many kinds of goods, including grain, oil, wine, fruits, spices, papyrus, and such luxury items as rich fabrics, jewels, and silver plates. These goods were taken ashore at the principal seaports of the western Mediterranean: Carthage, Ostia (near Rome), Marseilles, and Fos (Narbonne). The ships returned full of slaves, cloth, furs, weapons, such minerals as tin and silver, wood, grain, wine, wax, and cattle. It took about five days to go from Narbonne to Carthage, and a month to travel from Marseilles to Alexandria.

Ships also plied the Atlantic coast, the English Channel, and the North Sea. Numerous trade routes linked Spain, Gaul, Britain, and northern Europe. The seaports of Bordeaux, Nantes, Rouen, Quentovic (not far from Etaples), and Dorestad (in the Netherlands) exported the products of the Mediterranean, brought there by land and river routes, as well as the products of central Gaul. The Frisians and the Saxons, who were excellent sailors and merchants, became masters of the English Channel and the North Sea.

Overloaded with a cargo of grain and jars filled with pitch, a ship offers little resistance to a sudden storm. As it takes on water in the heavy seas sailors try in vain to pump out the hold. It is too late to right the vessel, and a shipwreck is inevitable, but the jetty of the seaport of Fos is very close.

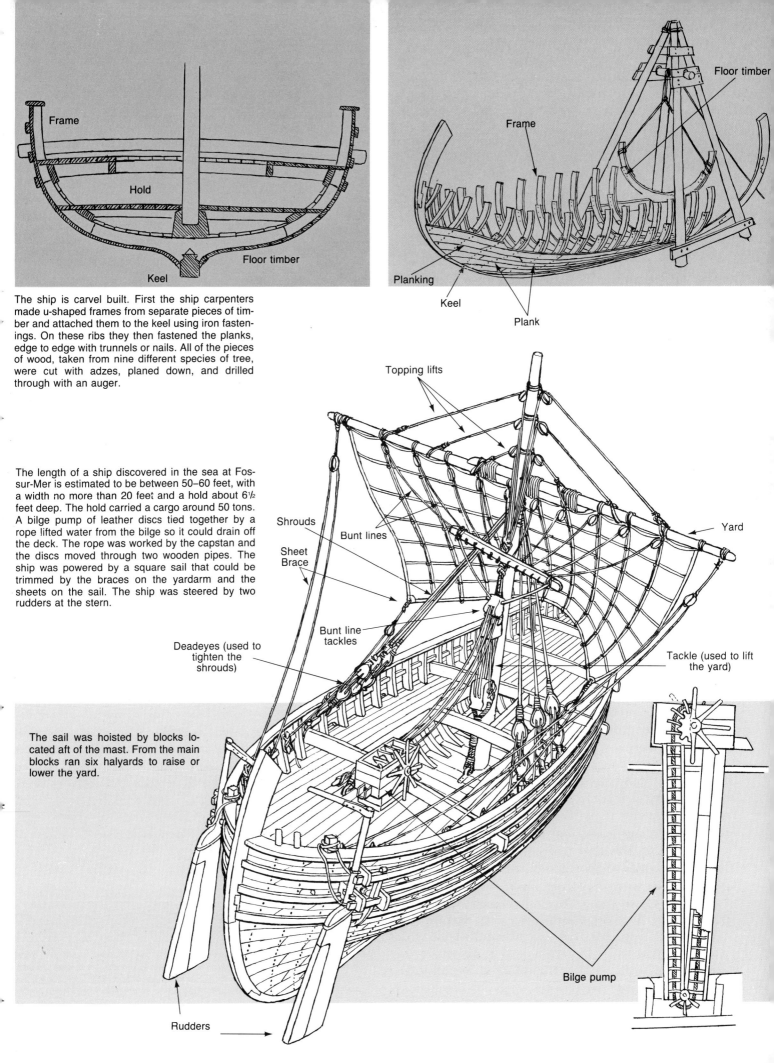

Frame

Hold

Floor timber

Keel

Frame

Floor timber

Planking

Keel

Plank

The ship is carvel built. First the ship carpenters made u-shaped frames from separate pieces of timber and attached them to the keel using iron fastenings. On these ribs they then fastened the planks, edge to edge with trunnels or nails. All of the pieces of wood, taken from nine different species of tree, were cut with adzes, planed down, and drilled through with an auger.

The length of a ship discovered in the sea at Fos-sur-Mer is estimated to be between 50–60 feet, with a width no more than 20 feet and a hold about 6½ feet deep. The hold carried a cargo around 50 tons. A bilge pump of leather discs tied together by a rope lifted water from the bilge so it could drain off the deck. The rope was worked by the capstan and the discs moved through two wooden pipes. The ship was powered by a square sail that could be trimmed by the braces on the yardarm and the sheets on the sail. The ship was steered by two rudders at the stern.

The sail was hoisted by blocks located aft of the mast. From the main blocks ran six halyards to raise or lower the yard.

Topping lifts

Shrouds

Bunt lines

Sheet
Brace

Yard

Bunt line
tackles

Deadeyes (used to
tighten the
shrouds)

Tackle (used to lift
the yard)

Bilge pump

Rudders

The Carolingian Renaissance

The period of the barbarian kingdoms has often been called the Dark Ages, in contrast with the Carolingian Renaissance. Actually, the relatively short-lived Carolingian civilization (from the middle of the eighth to the end of the tenth centuries) emerged for the most part from the Germano-Roman civilization of the barbarian epoch.

The Frankish Empire, more unified and stronger than before, dominated the greater part of Europe, its conquests due mainly to its formidable cavalry. It reached its height under Charlemagne, and extended from northern Spain and Italy to Saxony and the Danube. It had to confront the last invasions—those of the Vikings and Hungarians—while at the same time controlling Saxons, Slavs, Avars, Lombards, and Arabs. The great estates were managed better and benefited from technical innovations. The first fortified castles asserted the strength and independence of their owners in relation to the state, just as did the development of military and economic ties among men. Thus was born the system of lords and vassals so char-acteristic of the feudal world.

The Carolingian Renaissance was most apparent in cultural and artistic areas. Scientific and literary studies flourished, especially in the monasteries, where classical authors were rediscovered and schools multiplied. Sculpture, mosaics, frescoes, work in gold and ivory, and above all, illuminated manuscripts, are the most eloquent witnesses to this artistic renewal. To classic forms were added Byzantine and Anglo-Saxon influences.

As the heir of barbarian times, the Carolingian epoch laid the foundations of medieval civilization.

Charlemagne has returned to one of his favorite palaces, Ingelheim, near the banks of the Rhine. Accompanied by his royal suite, he enters the big semicircular court of honor. It is flanked by porticoes, and there is a covered well in the middle. All the buildings are of stone with brick foundations.

A cart moves along the road that leads to the celebrated abbey of Saint Gall. It is pulled easily by a horse wearing a horse collar on its shoulders. This innovation replaced the earlier collar, which, pressing against the throat, strangled the animal when the load was too heavy. A peasant works his field using a plow with an iron plowshare, wheels, and yoke. It is much more effective in digging a furrow than the old one, which did not penetrate deeply enough into the soil.

The charges of the Frankish cavalry are shattering, and dead Saracens are strewn across the plain at Poitiers. Protected effectively by a breastplate, helmet, and round shield, each horseman is armed with a heavy sword, a lance, and sometimes a bow. Because of a high saddle and stirrups, a horseman is one with his mount during a cavalry charge.

As the enemy army approaches, a castle prepares for attack. Soldiers take their places on the circular stone walls. In the center of the fortifications, a man-made mound of earth is topped by a square wooden keep. This is the home of the count, the master of the castle. It is perched over a bridge protected by a small log tower.

Following the Footsteps of the Barbarian Peoples

WRITTEN EVIDENCE AND THE DISCOVERIES OF ARCHAEOLOGY

It is because we have the evidence of texts and the discoveries of archaeology that we are able to write the history of the Great Invasions and the barbarian kingdoms. The same sources make it possible to present documentation for the original illustrations in this book.

The Written Witnesses

Contrary to what is often believed, writing played an important role in the early Middle Ages. Roman culture lived on, and there were both writers and copyists. Unfortunately, only a small portion of these writings has come down to us.

The rare authentic documents that have survived are public records (city charters, royal documents), and private records (bills of sale, wills, and so on) written on papyrus or parchment.

> DOCUMENT 1

Other writings are known through copies, some of them contemporary with the barbarian kingdoms. These include historical accounts, such as the History of the Franks *by Gregory of Tours and the* History of the Lombards *by Paul the Deacon, and literary works by Sidonius Apollinaris and Venantius Fortunatus. There are also innumerable lives of the saints, a type of writing much prized at the time.*

Liturgical works—psalms, gospels, and so on—were produced in the monasteries. Written in a beautiful, detailed script, they were adorned with the remarkable illustrations known as illuminations.

> DOCUMENT 2

Other written sources uncovered by archaeology, include coins, Christian epitaphs, and inscriptions on church furnishings.

> DOCUMENTS 3
> AND 4

Votive crown of Recceswinth, king of the Visigoths, seventh century. When it was made, this crown would have been hung in the cathedral at Toledo, Spain.
Diameter: 8 ins. (Archaeological Museum, Madrid)

1

Example of cursive writing in a Merovingian document

Derived from writing at the end of antiquity, Merovingian cursive writing can be read today only by specialists. This example of writing on parchment comes from a document dated June 20, 750, and is preserved in the French Archives. The first line contains the names of Pepin the Short's chief minister (*inluster vir Pippinus majoremdomus*), and of the palace of Attigny in the Ardennes (*Attiniaco in palacio publico*). Like all Merovingian documents, it is in Latin.

(Paris, Bibliothèque Nationale. Ms. Latin 12168, fol. 1)

3

The epitaph of Cheldofrida

In 1944 a beautiful epitaph was discovered in the church at Pier, near Düren in West Germany. The style of the letters, engraved on the stone, indicates that it was written in the seventh century. It bears the name of Lady Cheldofrida (DOMNA CHELDOF-RIDA), who died at the age of 45 (ANNUS XXXXV), fifteen days before the calends of February (POST DIES XV DE KALENDAS FEBRUARIUS)—which means January 18.

This inscription shows that, at a time of total domination by barbarians, the ancient form for epitaphs continued—written in Latin and using the traditional formulas, numbers, and Roman calendar. Antiquity was not dead!

(From K. Bohner. *Das Grab eines fränkischen Herren aus Morken im Rheinland,* Museum of the Rhine, Bonn, 1959.)

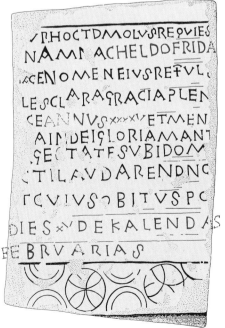

2

An Illuminated Manuscript

In the monasteries in the north and east of Gaul, the monks did not simply copy the sacred texts in careful calligraphy. They also illuminated them. They used beautiful colors for the designs—taken from architecture, geometry, and animal forms—with which they decorated their frontispieces and initial letters. This page on parchment, is a good example. It is a copy of a book by Saint Augustine and dates from the second half of the eighth century.

4

The historical message of coins

This small gold coin—a third of a sou—weighs less than $^1/_{10}$ ounce, but carries a historical message.

On one side, around a stylized royal portrait, runs the inscription PARISIUS IN CIVI(TAE). This means that the coin was minted at Paris, the capital of the Merovingians.

On the other side, around a cross, are the words CHLOD (OVIVS) REX and, under the cross, the word ELIGI. The coin, in the name of Clovis II (638–657), was struck by the celebrated goldsmith and minter, Saint Eligius, between 639 and 641.

A third of a sou represented one-ninth of the price of a young pig. It took 900 of these to compensate for having murdered a man in the prime of his life.

(Collection of the Carnavalet Museum, Paris; photo P. Pierrain.)

6

The "crypt" of Saint Paul of Jouarre

In the seventh century, Theodechilde, the Merovingian abbess of Jouarre (Seine-et-Marne), France, enlarged the mausoleum of her convent with new construction that was partly underground. She may have done so to honor her brother, Agilbert, who was bishop of Paris. (His sarcophagus, decorated with scenes of people at prayer, is at the left.) The founder of this celebrated convent, and the abbesses who succeeded her, were buried in this mausoleum. In time, cenotaphs (false decorative tombs) were placed on the stone coffins (at right).

The "crypt" of Saint Paul of Jouarre is rectangular. It is divided into three parts by rows of columns. The marble capitals, though in an original style, echo classical models.

(Photo F. Lontcho, Editions Errance.)

5

The baptistery of Poitiers

In Gaul, Italy, Spain, and North Africa, the architectural traditions of late antiquity continued during the barbarian epoch. The baptistery of Poitiers, built in the seventh century, is a good example. Its plan is in the form of a cross; its walls, of "small stone" construction, also include rows of bricks. Columns and capitals of marble complete the interior decoration.

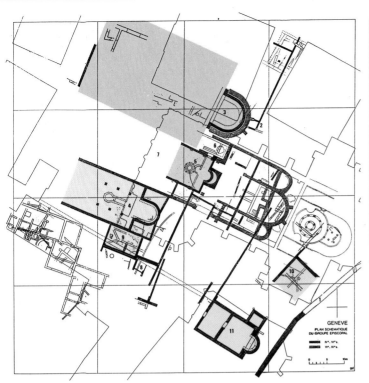

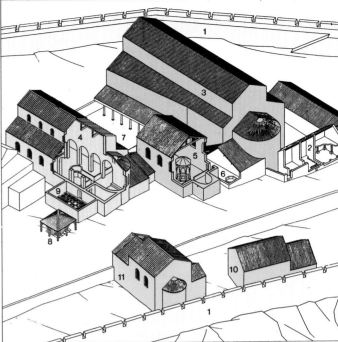

7

The bishop's quarters in Geneva

Extensive research and excavations, undertaken since 1979 at Saint Peter's Cathedral in Geneva, permit a very precise reconstruction of the bishop's quarters in the ancient Burgundian capital.

Investigation of the complex foundations revealed two churches, a baptistery, and various other buildings. The drawings show how this monumental architectural group probably looked in the fifth and sixth centuries.

1. The enclosing wall at the end of the Roman era. 2. A building of the Byzantine period. 3. The northern cathedral. 4. The southern cathedral. 5. The baptistery. 6. The secondary baptismal basin. 7. The atrium (a courtyard lined with columns). 8. The well. 9. The bishop's reception room. 10. Part of the bishop's residence. 11. The bishop's chapel.

(From C. Bonnet and G. Deuber, Cantonal Bureau of Archaeology of Geneva.)

The Discoveries of Archaeology

Archaeology is helpful in adding to the evidence of written texts, whether through the study of existing monuments or through the indispensable information provided by excavations.

The barbarians who settled in the Roman Empire in the West erected many religious monuments: cathedrals, baptisteries, mausoleums, monasteries, and so on. Several of them still exist, more or less well-preserved. In Gaul, for example, there are the baptistery of Poitiers, the mausoleum of the Abbé Mellebaude at Poitiers (an underground burial chamber), and the "crypt" of Saint Paul of Jouarre. They show the survival of classical architectural techniques.

DOCUMENTS **5** AND **6**

Other buildings, whose existence is known from written texts, have been discovered through excavation. Usually nothing remains but the foundations which reveal the floor plan of the building, and a few architectural elements. The latter include marble columns and capitals, beautifully carved liturgical screens such as that of the church of Saint-Pierre-aux-Nonnains at Metz, bricks, and decorative tiles and mosaics.

DOCUMENT **7**

Wood was used widely in northern Europe to build palaces, churches, and houses, both in the cities and in the country. Obviously nothing remains of these structures except traces in the earth (post holes or ditches, for instance). But careful excavation enables experts to discover traces and reconstruct the plans of these buildings.

DOCUMENT **8**

The excavation of cemeteries has provided the most spectacular and easily accessible evidence. It is possible to reconstruct the outward appearance of the cemeteries, with their enclosures and tombstones. And the study of skeletal remains (when bodies have not been cremated) reveals the measurements of the dead, their age at the time of death, some of the illnesses from which they suffered, and sometimes even their ethnic origins.

DOCUMENTS **9** AND **10**

Like a detective, the archaeologist can draw a social portrait of the dead: king, rich warrior, pauper, or slave. Personal objects left in the tombs help in the investigation and often make it possible to reconstruct the clothing of the period.

DOCUMENTS **11** AND **12**

The study of funeral practices also teaches us about religious beliefs.

Sometimes it seems as if the archaeologist is discovering a news item fifteen or sixteen centuries later: a warrior with a jaw smashed by a blow from a battle-ax; a mother who died in childbirth and was buried with her stillborn baby; a woman buried face down with her hands tied behind her back as punishment for some unknown crime.

Full archaeological analysis of cemeteries presents an even clearer picture of barbarian society and adds concrete details to written records.

Laboratory analysis of the numerous objects found in tombs (weapons, jewels, costume ornaments, vases) reveals the techniques that were used to make them. The geographical location of such objects allows scholars to identify the places where they were produced, as well as the most important trade routes. The excavation of potters' and metallurgists' workshops, as well as heaps of rubble, adds important information.

When we examine the ornamentation of statues, utensils, and illuminated manuscripts, we cannot help but admire the artistic sense of the barbarians, whether the themes are human, animal, vegetable, or geometric.

DOCUMENT 13

Although the discovery of new texts from the barbarian epoch is unlikely, archaeological discoveries occur all the time, and the possibilities created by new excavations are vast. Instead of being pursued as "treasure hunts," these investigations must be carried out scientifically to achieve an increasingly detailed historical understanding of the Great Invasions and the barbarian kingdoms.

Glass vase found at Douvrend (France), sixth century. Height: 4.8 inches. (Departmental Museum of Antiquities, Rouen, photo F. Dugué.)

Ostrogothic brooch of gold and enamel in the form of an eagle. Domagnano (Italy), first half of the sixth century. Height: 4.8 inches (British Museum, London).

Ornament of inlaid iron for a sword belt, found at Paris. Merovingian, first half of the seventh century. Length: 11.2 inches (Carnavalet Museum, Paris, photo P. Pierrain.)

Anglo-Saxon round brooch of gold and enamel, Kingstone Down, Great Britain, about 600. Diameter: 3.4 inches. (Liverpool Museum.)

Merovingian belt buckle cast in bronze, around the year 600. Length: 3.6 inches (Carnavalet Museum, Paris, photo P. Pierrain.)

Merovingian brooch in the form of an ankh (a cross with a loop at the top), made of gilded silver, found at Douvrend (France). Height: 5.6 inches. (Departmental Museum of Antiquities, Rouen, photo F. Dugué.)

The Frankish village at Gladbach

Excavations in 1936 at Gladbach, near the Rhine city of Neuwied, (West Germany) revealed for the first time the exact layout of a Frankish village. Stripping away the soil revealed blotches of color darker than that of the surrounding earth. They corresponded to post holes, trenches, and pits, which archaeologists interpreted accordingly.

Divided into sections by fences, the village was made up of houses and other buildings.

The walls and roofs of the houses which were built directly on the ground, were kept in place by many poles. Smaller buildings—merely huts constructed over pits—were supported by just two, four, or six poles. These little structures served as stables, cowsheds, or workshops.

(From W. Sage, *Die fränkische Siedlung bei Gladbach,* museum of the Rhine, Bonn, 1969.)

8

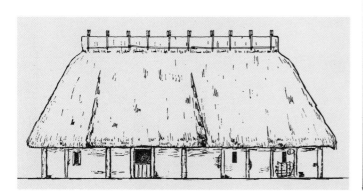

▲
Reconstruction of a house: framework and exterior appearance.
▼

Reconstruction of a hut: exterior appearance.

Simplified plan of Frankish village at Gladbach.

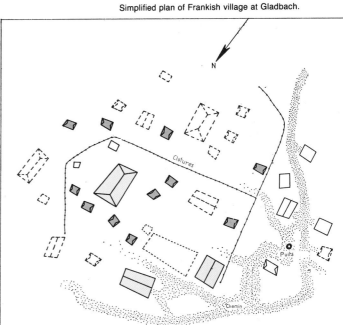

The Alemanni cemetery at Fridlingen

9

The Alemanni cemetery at Fridlingen, in southeast Germany, was systematically excavated in 1971. Archaeologists were able to reconstruct the appearance of the cemetery when it was used during the seventh and eighth centuries.

Most of the tombs were marked by nothing more than small mounds of earth showing the alignment of the graves. At one end of the huge cemetery, many tumuli (large mounds) stood over the tombs of the upper classes, isolating them from the rest of the population.

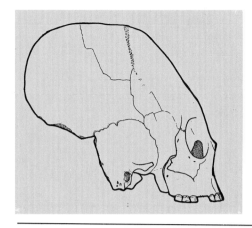

10

An example of the artificial deformation of a skull

One of the skeletons brought to light in the barbarian cemetery at Briord in eastern France near Geneva had a skull with a strange shape. The cranium had been artificially deformed in infancy by a band tied tightly around it.

We know through other archaeological examples that this custom, practically unknown among the Franks and Alemanni, was practiced by the Huns and the eastern Germans. They transmitted it to the Burgundians during the period of their kingdom at Worms (until 436). The Burgundians then settled in eastern Gaul (beginning in 443), where they continued this practice for some time. The Briord cranium offers an eloquent illustration of the migration of this Germanic people. It also shows how much the study of bones, part of the science of anthropology, contributes to historical understanding.

(From St. Gaillard de Semainville, et. al. in *La Physiophile*, No. 88, 1978, Montceau-les-Mines.)

The tomb of a Frankish "noble" at Morken

Excavations of the foundations of the church of Saint Morken, near Cologne, West Germany, led to the discovery in 1955 of several Frankish tombs. One of them, exceptional for its large size and rich contents, was that of a high-ranking warrior, now called, for want of a better title, the "noble" or "chief."

Based on their excavations, archaeologists were able to reconstruct what the tomb looked like at the time it was prepared, about the year 600. A large funeral chamber was dug and lined with heavy beams. The deceased was placed in a heavy wooden coffin, which was placed along one of the chamber walls. Dressed in his finest clothing, the "noble" of Morken had his sword at his side. His shield was placed between

11

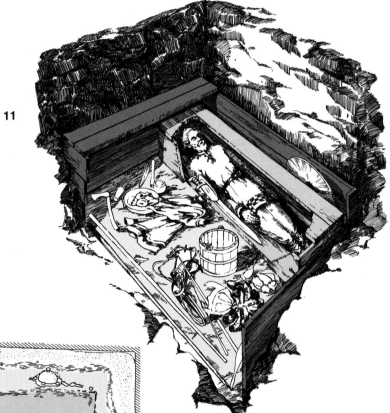

the coffin and the chamber wall. On the other side of the coffin were laid out carefully some of the things most precious to the deceased: a fish spear, a lance, a boar spear, a battle-ax, a helmet, the bit from the bridle of his horse, a bronze basin and a napkin (proof of a refined way of life), a glass goblet, a pottery vase and a wooden pail and cover.

(From K. Bohner, *Das Grab eines fränkischen Herren aus Morken,* Museum of the Rhine, Bonn, 1959.)

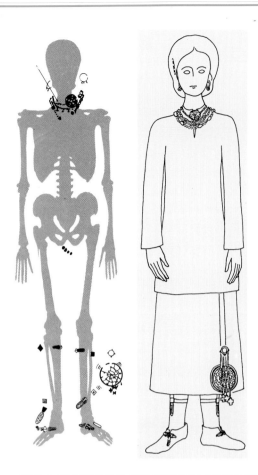

12

A fashionable woman of the seventh century: the Lady of Bülach

While excavating at the Church of Saint Lawrence in Bülach, Switzerland, diggers uncovered the foundations of an earlier church. This small rectangular building measured only 56 feet long and 23 feet wide. In the middle they found the tomb of a wealthy woman, probably the founder of this place of worship. She had died in about the year 650.

Because the archaeologists excavated so carefully, they were able to work out an exact reconstruction of the woman's clothing based on the position of her jewelry and accessories on her clothes. In the fashion of the Alemanni of the period, the Lady of Bülach wore a long hairpin, as well as earrings, a brooch at her throat, and several short necklaces. A purse with a bronze clasp and pendants in the form of crosses (the lady was a Christian) hung from her belt down to her calf. Her skirt ended halfway down her leg, showing the ornaments on the garters that held up her stockings. Her shoes were fastened with metal buckles.

(From R. Christlein, *Die Alamannen*, Stuttgart, 1968.)

13

Understanding animal motifs

It is not always easy to make sense of barbarian decorative design. The first impression is often that of a tangle of jumbled, sinuous lines. With practice, however, it is possible to recognize simple symmetrical compositions depicting very stylized animals. There are, for example, the heads of eagles and wild boars (the latter recognizable by their tusks) surrounding a human mask on the pendant of a belt found at Wurmlingen, West Germany.

(From W. Hubener, *Die Goldblattkreuze des frühen Mittelalters*, the Alemanni Institute of Friburg in Brisgau, 1975.)

SOURCES

The original gouaches of Pierre Joubert have been carefully documented. Below you will find, in the form of a bibliography, a list of the principal books that were used in the choice of scenes represented in the 23 chapters of this book. The artists also used a number of specialized archaeological journals in order to reconstruct, with the greatest possible degree of historical truth, both settings and costumes; *each illustration corresponds to a particular period or a precise place. The authors also give below, chapter by chapter, some references to particular sources: texts of the period (for example, the* History of the Franks *by Gregory of Tours = H.F.), modern publications, and the names of experts who were kind enough to make available to the authors very valuable documentation, often unpublished.*

Pages 14–15

Reconstruction of the Roman Forum based on a model of Rome in the fourth century (Museum of Roman Civilization, Rome).

Based on the excavation of Jean-Pierre LEMANT at Mont-Vireux (Ardennes), France.

Dominating the Sarthe River, the base of the ancient wall is still visible at Le Mans, France.

One can still see at Turnu Severin, Rumania, the vestiges of the camp, as well as the piles of the old Roman bridge across the Danube.

Pages 16–17

The Christian emblem (the Lombards were Arians), with a dove surmounting a cross, is based on a Lombard figurine of a flag bearer, done in bronze (From I. BONA, *Gépides et Lombards*, Budapest, 1976).

Based on the account by Priscus. The wife of Attila actually lived in a nearby palace, just as luxurious, where the Greek writer saw her reclining on a woolen carpet and surrounded by her ladies-in-waiting. Attila had stone baths built in the vicinity, copying the practice of the Romans.

Pages 18–19

The scene takes place among the Alemanni.

The royal archives were carefully classified, as indicated by classification marks on the reverse of certain documents preserved at the National Archives in Paris. These marks, visible when the documents of papyrus or parchment were rolled up, allowed them to be easily retrieved.

Based on Gregory of Tours, *H.F.*, V. 28.

Id., IV, 22.

Pages 20–21

The costume and arms of the king are based on Rupert BRUCE-MITFORD (*The Sutton Hoo Ship Burial*, London, 1972.) The king was buried at Sutton Hoo (East Anglia) in a ship transformed into a burial mound in the Scandinavian manner. The tomb was excavated on the eve of World War II. Its marvelous contents are displayed at London in the British Museum.

Numbers 1 and 4: based on Michael KAZANSKI; number 2: based on Falko DAIM (graveyard at Leobersdorf, Austria); number 3: based on G. LASZLO *Steppenvölker und Germanen*, Vienna-Munich, 1970; number 5: based on P. PAULSEN (graveyard at Niederstötzingen, West Germany); number 6: based on O. von HESSEN (graveyard at Testona, Italy); number 7: based on the tome of Childeric (publication by J.-J. CHIFLET, 1955). Some of these objects are on display at Paris, in the Medal Collection of the Bibliothèque National.

Pages 22–23

This battle was the origin of the legendary *Nibelungenlied,* which inspired Richard Wagner, among others.

Based on a document in the Landesmuseum of Stuttgart (West Germany): R. WOLF, *Das frühe Mittelalter SCHWABEN UND FRANKEN.*

Pages 24–25

Based on Gregory of Tours, *H.F.,* VIII, 15. New converts helped the stylite (a hermit living on top of a column) overturn and smash a statue of Diana. The small hermitage was then replaced by a great church admired by Gregory of Tours. There were many stylites in the East, but Saint Walfroy was the only one in the West.

Tradition says that a manuscript preserved in the Abbey of Fulda, West Germany, founded by a disciple of Saint Boniface, was the prayer book with which he tried to defend himself. Its cover does in fact show the mark of a sword thrust.

Reconstruction based on the plans of J. MARTENS, in *Archaeologica Belgica,* vol. 61.

Pages 26–27

Based on Gregory of Tours, *H.F.,* VII, 37. Existing town of Saint-Bertrand-de-Comminges (Haute-Garonne), France.

The liturgical screen that separates the area occupied by the clergy at the altar (the chancel) from the faithful was inspired by that of the church of Saint-Pierre-aux-Nonnains at Metz, France, displayed in the Archaeological Museum of that city.

Based on Gregory of Tours, *H.F.,* VIII, 33.

Id., VIII, 31. This event took place in the year 586.

Id., VI, 31. This disaster occurred in 563.

Pages 28–29

Based on Gregory of Tours, *To The Glory of Confessors,* 77.

Based on Gregory of Tours, *H.F.,* VI, 35.

Based on Gregory of Tours, *To The Glory of Confessors,* 2.

Based on the *Life of Barbatus, Bishop of Benevent.* This event took place in the middle of the seventh century.

Based on May VIEIL-LARD-TROIEKOUROFF,

Les monuments religieux de la Gaule d'après les oeuvres de Grégoire de Tours, Paris, 1976.

Pages 30–31

This manuscript from Corbie (Somme), France, dating from the second half of the eighth century, is preserved at the Bibliothèque Nationale in Paris.

On Valerius (died 695), see C. M. AHERNE, *Valerio of Bierzo, an Ascetic of the Late Visigothic Period,* Washington, 1949.

Pages 32–33

This scene took place among the Alemanni, between the Black Forest and Lake Constance. Clothing is based on R. MOOSBRUGGER-LEU *Die Schweiz zur Merowingerzeit,* Berne, 1971, and R. Christlein, *Die Alamannen,* Stuttgart, 1978.

Based on Gregory of Tours, *H.F.,* X, 8.

The baptismal font was usually covered by a roof (a *ciborium*) resting on small columns.

Pages 34–35

Based on an interpretation by J-P. LAPORTE in *Bulletin du Groupement Archéologique de Seine-et-Marne,* 1982, 23.

Number 1: based on M. FLEURY and A. FRANCE-LANORD, in *Germania,* 1962, 40 (tomb discovered in the basilica of Saint Denis in 1959 and attributed to Queen Aregonde, the wife of Clotaire I); number 2: based on O. DOPPEL-FELD, in *Germania,* 1960, 38 (pp. 44–45) (tomb of the "Lady of Cologne"); numbers 3, 5 and 9: based on documents from Michael KAZANSKI; number 4: based on Edmond SERVAT (recent excavations at the cemetery of Vicq, Yvelines, France) and A. MOLINARO PEREZ (*La Necropolis Visigoda de Duraton, Segovia,* Madrid, 1948); numbers 6 and 7: based on R. CHRISTLEIN and R. MOOSBRUGGER-LEU, mentioned above (pp. 32–33); number 8: based on I. BONA, mentioned above (pp. 16–17); number 10: based on J. YPEY, in *Studien zur Sachsenforschung,* 1977 (tomb of the "princess" of Zweeloo, Netherlands).

Pages 36–37

Based on Gregory of Tours, *H.F.,* VIII, 36.

Pages 38–39

Based on the publication of K. Büohner, *Das Grab eines Fränkischen Herren aus Morken in Rheinland,* Cologne, 1959.

The stone sarcophagus is the type used in Burgundy-Champagne, France.

Based on the excavations of the Merovingian cemetery at Vorges (Aisne), France.

Based on X. BARRAL I. ALTET, in *Atti del IX Congressio internazionale di Archeologia cristiana,* Rome, 1978.

Pages 40–41

Based on the excavations of P.-H. Giot on the island of Guennoc, on the north coast of Brittany, France: (*Les premiers Bretons,* Châteaulin, 1982).

Pages 42–43

Based on a reconstruction of the village of Warendorf in Westphalia (seventh-eighth centuries) by W. WINKELMANN, *Neue Ausgrabungen in Deutschland,* 1958.

Based on the poem by Venantius Fortunatus (d. 600), *La Moselle,* written in 565 or 566.

Pages 44–45

Based on Gregory of Tours, *H.F.,* VIII, 42.

Based on the recent excavations of ecclesiastical buildings at Lyons, France, by Jean-François REYNAUD.

The dress of the duchess was inspired by that of the "Lady of Cologne," discovered in 1959 under the cathedral of that city (publication by O. DOPPELFELD, in *Germania,* 1960, 38). The scene is described by Gregory of Tours, *H.F.,* IX, 9.

Pages 46–47

Based on investigations and documents by Philippe ANDRIEUX. Site of the workshops of Huy, Belgium, after J. WILLEMS, *Archaeologica Belgica,* 1973, 148.

Pages 48–49

Based on investigations and documents by Jaap YPEY (National Service of Excavations of the Netherlands, at Amersfoort).

Based on investigations and documents by Philippe ANDRIEUX (departmental archaeologist, Val-de-Marne, France)

Based on investigations in 1981 at the Carnavalet Museum, Paris, which has the most important collection of Merovingian sarcophagi in decorated plaster (documentation by P. PERIN and C. COLLOT, Lambert Industries).

Based on terra cotta architectural remains at the Carnavalet Museum, Paris.

Based on documents provided by G-R. DELAHAYE. The face of the rock, showing the marks of the blocks earmarked for sarcophagi, is still visible in the quarry at Arcy-sur-Cure (Yonne), France.

Based on the reconstruction in an open-air park, of a house excavated at West Stow (Suffolk, England): *Sachsen und Angelsachsen,* catalogue of the Helms Museum of Hamburg, 1978.

Pages 52–53

Reconstruction of the basilica of Saint Denis, Paris, in the eighth century after S. Mc CROSBY.

Based on documentation of Philippe ANDRIEUX.

Pages 54–55

Based on the *Miracles de Saint Martin,* IV, 17.

Based on Gregory of Tours, *H.F.,* VII, 35.

Pages 56–57

Based on documents and suggestions by Marie-Pierre JEZEGOU, director of the underwater excavation of a Merovingian ship sunk at Fos-sur-Mer in the seventh century (Bouches-du-Rhône), France.

Pages 58–59

Based on excavations of the palace at Ingelheim and the reconstruction by C. RAUCH and H.-J. JACOBI, *Ausgrabungen in der Königspfalz Ingelheim,* Mainz, 1976. Vestiges of the palace are still visible in the little town of Ingelheim, near Mainz, West Germany.

Silhouette of the Abbey of Saint Gall, Switzerland, after the model by W. BORN, C.-B. LUND and S. KARSCHUNKE, an exact reproduction of a famous plan dating from the beginning of the ninth century (Stiftsbibliothek of Saint-Gall, Switzerland).

Weapons and armor constructed based on archaeology and illuminated manuscripts of the Carolingian epoch: Bible of Vivien, said to be that of Charles the Bald (845–846), and the Gospels of Lothair (between 849 and 851), Bibliothèque Nationale, Paris.

Based on excavations of the residence of the Count of Douai (Nord), France: built between 950 and 1100 (P. DEMOLON, *Douai, une ville face à son passé,* Douai, 1982).

Chronological Tableau of Principal Events (From 378 to 756)

NORTH AFRICA	ASIA BYZANTINE EMPIRE	ITALY	SPAIN	GAUL	BRITAIN
	378 Roman defeat at Adrianople Goths invade the Empire **395** Death of Emperor Theodosius	**410** Rome captured by Alaric, king of the Visigoths **423** Death of Emperor Honorius **440–461** Pope Leo I	**409** Invasion by Alani, Suevi, and Vandals **484** Visigoths invade	**404–407** Invasions by Alani, Suevi, and Vandals **412** Visigoths in the south **443** Burgundians in French and Swiss Jura Mountains **451** Defeat of Attila near Troyes	**About 407** Evacuation by Roman forces
429 Vandal invasion **439** Capture of Carthage	**453** Death of Attila		**470** Hegemony of the Visigoths	**482** Rise of Clovis **507** Victory of Clovis over the Visigoths **511** Death of Clovis and division of his kingdom among his four sons	**450** Invasion of Angles and Saxons. Britons flee west and cross the Channel into Armorica
477 Death of King Genseric		**476** End of Roman Empire in the West **493** Victory of Theodoric over Odoacer		**534** End of Burgundian kingdom **536** Franks in Provence	
523–530 Reign of Hilderic **533** Carthage taken by Byzantine general, Belisarius. End of Vandal kingdom	**527–565** Reign of Emperor Justinian	**526** Death of Theodoric Rule of St. Benedict **535** Byzantines in Sicily **541–552** Totila, king of the Ostrogoths	**531** Appearance of the Ostrogoth Theudis, who defeats Franks and Byzantines **550** Conversion of Suevi		**550** Anglo-Saxons resume attack on Britons
	567 Avars in Europe	**555** End of Ostrogothic kingdom **568** Lombard invasion **583** Death of writer Cassiodorus **590–604** Pope Gregory I **615** Death of Saint Colomban at Bobbio	**567** Leovigild becomes king **589** Conversion of Reccared. Visigoths abandon Arianism and convert to Catholicism	**558–561** Clotaire I unites Gaul **561–584** Reign of Childeric I **About 594** Death of Gregory of Tours **613** King Clotaire II **628–639** King Dagobert. Merovingian Gaul reunified	**597** Augustine, missionary in England. Conversion of Athelbert, king of Kent **617** Supremacy of Northumbrian kingdom **653** Supremacy of Mercia
647 First Arab invasion **698** Arabs capture Carthage	**632** Death of Mohammed **642** Arabs capture Alexandria **669** First siege of Byzantium by Arabs **717** Second siege of Byzantium **730** Edict against religious images	**643** Edict of Rothari codifying national customs of Lombards. **713** King Liutprand **749** King Aistolf **751** Lombards capture Ravenna **754** Victories of Pepin over the Lombards Franks establish first Papal State **774** Charlemagne, king of the Lombards	**636** Death of writer Isidore of Seville **654** Edict of Receswinth ends Romano-Visigothic differences **711** Arab invasion	**714** Death of Pepin of Heristal **732** Battle of Poitiers ends Muslim advance into Europe **751** King Pepin. Rise of the Carolingians **754** Death of Pope Boniface	**664** Synod of Whitby. Celtic clergy recognizes authority of Rome **709** Death of King Aldhelm **735** Death of the Venerable Bede

Glossary

Abbey The group of buildings in which a group of monks or nuns live, work, and pray.

Allies Countries or groups of people who are united with each other during a war.

Archaeology The study of the people, customs, and life during ancient times.

Architecture The science or art of building.

Aristocracy The upper class.

Armaments The supplies and weapons needed to wage a war.

Artisan A skilled workman who practices a trade

Cavalry Soldier or warriors who fight on horseback.

Commerce Business dealings.

Convent The building in which a group of nuns live.

Conversion To change from one belief or faith to another.

Cremate To burn a dead body to ashes.

Crypt A room or vault located underground. Often used for burials.

Cuirass A piece of armor used to protect the torso; a breastplate.

Damascene The technique of decorating metal with wavy inlaid or etched patterns.

Deities Gods or goddesses.

Empire A number of countries all governed by the same ruler. The ruler of an empire is called an emperor.

Epidemic A serious, often fatal disease that spreads rapidly and is contracted by many people at the same time.

Famine A lack of food, a time of hunger.

Fresco A painting on a wall or ceiling. Paint is applied to the surface when the plaster is damp so that the colors sink into the plaster.

Funeral pyre The pile of wood upon which a body is burned as part of a funeral rite.

Heresy A belief that does not go along with the accepted beliefs of a religion. A person who holds such a belief is called a heretic.

Illuminated manuscript A book that has been decorated with pictures and designs done in gold, silver, and bright colors.

Infrastructure The most important parts of a structure or system.

Martyr Someone who submits to suffering or even death rather than go back on their beliefs or deny their religion.

Mercenary A person who is paid to fight for a foreign government or ruler.

Migration The act of moving from one area and settling in another.

Missionary A person who is sent out to spread Christian religion.

Monastery A building in which a group of monks live.

Mosaic A picture or design that has been made with small pieces of glass or stone

Nomad A member of a wandering tribe that moves from one place to another in search of food, grazing land for livestock, and the means to live.

Pagan Someone who is a follower of a religion other than a Christian religion.

Pilgrimage A journey made to a holy place or shrine.

Pillage To rob violently.

Plunder To rob and loot.

Renaissance A rebirth of art, literature, and thought.

Saint Someone who has been canonized.

Sarcophagus A coffin made of stone, often decorated with ornamental sculptures.

Seneschal Someone who was in charge of an estate or royal palace. Their power was frequently similar to judges' or generals'.

Smith Someone who makes things out of metal.

Soothsayer Someone who can predict future events.

Tomb A place of burial.

Tribunal A court of justice.

Villa A large, elegant house in the country.

Index